The death of Fr John I

Maynooth Studies in Local History

SERIES EDITOR Raymond Gillespie

This volume is one of six short books published in the Maynooth Studies in Local History series in 2010. Like over 85 of their predecessors they range widely over the local experience in the Irish past. That local experience is presented in the complex social world of which it is part, from the world of the dispossessed Irish in 17th-century Donegal to political events in 1830s Carlow; from the luxury of the early 19th-century Dublin middle class to the poverty of the Famine in Tipperary; and from the political activists in Kimmage in 1916 to those who suffered in a different sort of war as their homes were bombed in South Circular Road in 1941. These local experiences cannot be a simple chronicling of events relating to an area within administrative or geographically determined boundaries since understanding the local world presents much more complex challenges for the historian. It is a reconstruction of the socially diverse worlds of poor and rich as well as those who took very different positions on the political issues that preoccupied the local societies of Ireland. Reconstructing such diverse local worlds relies on understanding of what the people of the different communities that made up the localities of Ireland had in common and what drove them apart. Understanding the assumptions, often unspoken, around which these local societies operated is the key to recreating the world of the Irish past and reconstructing the way in which those who inhabited those worlds lived their daily lives. As such, studies such as those presented in these short books, together with their predecessors, are at the forefront of Irish historical research and represent some of the most innovative and exciting work being undertaken in Irish history today. They also provide models which others can follow up and adapt in their own studies of the Irish past. In such ways will we understand better the regional diversity of Ireland and the social and cultural basis for that diversity. If they also convey something of the vibrancy and excitement of the world of Irish local history today they will have achieved at least some of their purpose.

Maynooth Studies in Local History: Number 92

The death of Fr John Walsh at Kilgraney
Community tensions in pre-Famine Carlow

Maura Cronin

FOUR COURTS PRESS

Set in 10pt on 12pt Bembo by
Carrigboy Typesetting Services for
FOUR COURTS PRESS LTD
7 Malpas Street, Dublin 8, Ireland
www.fourcourtspress.ie
and in North America for
FOUR COURTS PRESS
c/o ISBS, 920 N.E. 58th Avenue, Suite 300, Portland, OR 97213.

ISBN 978–1–84682–263–6

Printed in Scotland
by Thomson Litho, Glasgow.

Contents

Acknowledgments

I wish to thank Professor Raymond Gillespie for the welcome invitation to contribute to the Maynooth Studies in Local History, and for his incomparable patience in waiting for me to produce the finished piece. I would also like to mark my gratitude to the staffs of the National Archives, Mary Immaculate College Library, Limerick, and the Local Studies Library, Carlow, for their helpfulness in the course of my research. I am also greatly indebted to two Carlow historians. One is Michael Brennan who, in an all too brief conversation over a microfilm reader in the Carlow library, gave me some excellent insights into a number of the protagonists in the Kilgraney affair. The other is the late Tom Murphy. Well on in my research I discovered his wonderful compilation of historical material concerning the priest at the centre of this story, and though the discovery came late, it presented me with evidence that I could not otherwise have found. Finally, I have to say the biggest thanks of all to my husband and family for their willingness to play second fiddle for all too long to Fr John Walsh of Borris.

1. A body at Kilgraney

On Sunday, 1 August 1936, a crowd of around a thousand people gathered at Kilgraney bridge, just four miles from the Co. Carlow town of Borris, to witness the unveiling of a large Celtic cross, the foundation stone of which had been laid during a similar ceremony a year previously. The unveiling was performed by a local priest, and on the platform were several public figures – TDs, County Councillors with a large group of clergy – from Carlow and the neighbouring counties of Wexford and Kilkenny. Local bands played 'Faith of Our Fathers' and the national anthem, while the oration, delivered by a Wexford TD, lauded Ireland's adherence to the Catholic faith over the centuries, even in the present age when 'a godless revolution' gripped other countries.[1]

The individual honoured on the occasion was Fr John Walsh, the Roman Catholic curate of Borris, whose dead body was found early on the morning of 31 July 1835 near Kilgraney bridge. The priest had apparently died from head injuries and the spattered bloodstains on the ditch and the bridge parapet suggested that his death had been traumatic, though whether through another's agency or simply by falling heavily against the parapet was not clear. It was estimated that the priest's death had occurred about an hour before midnight on 30 July, since shortly after ten o'clock he had left another priest's house at Bagnalstown, to ride home to Borris, and Kilgraney was about three miles from Bagenalstown – about a twenty minute journey for a cantering horse. This timing was supported in the evidence of a man who, while driving a horse and car to the colliery on the night of the priest's death, had passed by Kilgraney bridge around eleven o'clock. He and his companion had seen a bulk on the road and heard groaning, but thinking that it was a man in a drunken stupor had not stopped to investigate as they 'did not like to have anything to do with the like' lest they be accused afterwards of robbery.[2]

How had Walsh died? There were three possible simple explanations. One was that he had been thrown from a 'starting' or shying horse, which a number of witnesses believed to have thrown him before, one of his fellow priests reputedly remarking on the morning of the inquest: 'I knew that horse would be the death of him'.[3] Another explanation was that due to the darkness of the night and Walsh's own short sightedness (he wore glasses with a blue tinge), he had not realized he had reached the right-angled turn at Kilgraney bridge and his last-minute effort to take the corner had caused the horse to shy. The third explanation, favoured by those who were unsympathetic to priests, was that Walsh had been drunk, and therefore incapable of controlling the horse. However, a more sinister explanation of the tragedy was that there had been a murder – nothing unusual in the very disturbed decade of the 1830s. But if Walsh had been murdered, the question was: why and by whom? Obviously the motive had not been robbery, as Walsh's watch and a sum of thirteen shillings were still on his person. Nor was it considered to be one of the agrarian murders so common at the time, since Walsh was not involved in any land-related transactions. In the absence of obvious material motivations, it was quickly assumed that what was involved here was a political or sectarian murder, and it 'logically' followed that local Protestants were responsible, the finger being pointed at three Protestant farmers from two neighbouring townlands – Archibald Sly of Carrignafecca, and Abraham Wynne and Hugh Styles of Sliguff.[4]

In a county that was renowned for its sectarian tensions, this development caused major excitement, and sides were taken along predictably denomi- national lines in a controversy that dragged out for over three years. Things moved slowly at first since there was no conclusive evidence to warrant the immediate apprehension of Sly, Wynne and Styles, and though Archibald Sly was arrested within a month of Walsh's death, he had to be released again until more reliable evidence caused him to be committed to prison in mid- November 1835. Denied bail due to the seriousness of the charge against him, Sly stood trial at the following spring assizes in a Carlow that buzzed with speculation and anticipation, but he was acquitted when the stories of the main witnesses for the prosecution were seriously undermined under cross- examination.[5] The saga did not end here since, determined to pay back those who had landed him in prison, Sly immediately turned the tables on his opponents by bringing a successful counter-charge of perjury against some of those who had testified against him, and the drama closed fourteen months after Walsh's death with the transportation of three individuals, Hugh Corrigan, James Doyle and Anne Rooney.[6]

But the Kilgraney affair affected more than those immediately involved, and more than one small corner of a small Irish county. Its roots lay not just in local animosities but in a contest between larger forces that faced each other down in the reforming decade of the 1830s. Its repercussions, too, went beyond the fourteen months of its enactment and beyond the immediate regional arena, intensifying the conflict between political traditionalism and reformism.

JOHN WALSH AND ARCHIBALD SLY

His death at Kilgraney brought John Walsh a fame he would hardly have achieved otherwise. The unfolding of his life up to then is obscure, and the work of dedicated local historians has only unearthered the barest of details.[7] Walsh was born around 1800 in Grange Upper, probably attended Carlow College, and was ordained in 1822.[8] He served as curate to his uncle, another John, the politically active parish priest of Borris, Co. Carlow with whom he operated something of an uncle-nephew team in both parish and political affairs over the course of a decade. Typical of the emerging Irish Catholic priesthood of his day, he was drawn from the strong farming class and so, like his fellow priests, was of a different social order to most of his parishioners. This social gap was a result of both economic progress and church reform. As the fortunes of strong farmers improved, Catholic ecclesiastical authorities at home and in Rome forged the clergy into a separate caste, distinctively dressed, living apart from the generality of the population, and moving socially in their own increasingly exclusive circles. In the diocese of Kildare and Leighlin, where Borris was situated, this creation of a disciplined and distinctive clerical caste was fostered by Bishop James Doyle. Walsh, whose priestly career coincided with the last decade of Doyle's episcopacy, seems to have been a typical product of this reform, and his movements on the day of his death provide a brief but telling glimpse of the social and religious activities of the rural Catholic clergy in the mid-19th century.[9] Early on the morning of Thursday, 30 July, Walsh picked the most spirited of his horses and rode from Borris to Carlow to conclude some business, possibly in preparation for his journey to London the following day. He was to give evidence before a parliamentary committee on a highly controversial election that had been held a month previously, and in which the local landlords, Henry Bruen and Thomas Kavanagh, had been defeated by O'Connellite candidates. Some accounts said his visit to Carlow was to make a religious retreat (quite feasible in view of Bishop Doyle's clerical reforms), but this would hardly have been completed in a single day, though Walsh may well have taken the opportunity to attend the sacraments in preparation for his journey.[10] His journeys to Carlow and homewards that evening give an indication of the social circle he and his fellow priests inhabited. In the morning he rode to Bagenalstown, where he left his horse at the house of Fr James Nolan who brought him in his gig as far as Clogrenan Wood, the residence of Colonel Rochford just outside Carlow town. There they parted, Nolan attending a party at an unspecified house near Clogrenan while Walsh continued into Carlow where he dined and did his business. On the return journey, the two priests met up again at Clogrenan, went on to the house of Fr Kehoe at Leighlinbridge where they chatted briefly and drank a toast in negus (a mixture of claret, madeira, port and brandy). They then returned to Bagnalstown before Walsh resumed his fatal trip on horseback toward Borris *via* Kilgraney bridge.[11]

The other main character in the drama was Archibald Sly of Carricknafecca, a townland some five miles north-west of Kilgraney bridge and just over three miles west of Borris. An older man than Walsh, Sly was described as being 'about fifty years of age', and had lived in the immediate area of Borris for at least a decade – though possibly for much longer. If Walsh typified the Catholic clergy of his day, Sly was characteristic of a large number of substantial Protestant tenants in south Carlow. He was considered to belong to 'the better order of farmers', with a reputed annual property valuation of £200.[12] The acreage of his farm at Carricknafecca is unclear, but his registration as a £20 freeholder indicates that it was of good quality land and it may even have extended to as much as 100 acres.[13] Sly was prosperous enough to employ two live-in workmen, and was involved in sheep breeding on a commercial scale. Besides his substantial tenancy at Carrignafecca, he seems also to have recently acquired land at Sliguff near Kilgraney, where he was in the process of building or renovating a house at the time of Walsh's death.[14]

Walsh and Sly had much in common economically, with their roots in strong farming stock and their relative prosperity. Here, however, the similarities ended, since they were polar opposites in terms of the religious and political controversies of the day. Walsh represented an increasingly assertive and prosperous Catholic clergy. His socializing with other priests, his familiarity with genteel drinks like negus, and his horsemanship and ownership of several horses all marked Walsh off as belonging to a caste that was socially far above the *cosmhuintir*, and not very far behind the landed gentry. Sly typified the more modest members of the Protestant elite that, despite their material advancement were in immediate danger of social and political slippage in the reforming decade of the 1830s. The two men may actually never have met one another personally – and that is precisely what Sly and other Protestant farmers claimed. But because they so clearly represented two diametrically opposed groups, the alleged crossing of their paths came to be seen, even by contemporaries, as a microcosm of larger political and social conflicts. Thus, though the Kilgraney tragedy and its immediate aftermath were played out over some twenty townlands and an area of about six by four miles in extent, the suspicious death of a Catholic priest in an age of economic, sectarian and political tension was bound to start a quest for a scapegoat, and to cause controversy well beyond the local arena.

2. The Castle and the Walsh case

The 1830s was a decade of what contemporaries termed 'party spirit'. By this they meant the contest between two opposing forces. On one side were the defenders of Protestant hegemony (the landed elite, their retainers and the Established Church), described variously in the present work, as in the 1830s, as conservatives, ultra-Protestants, and upholders of Protestant ascendancy. On the other side was an increasingly assertive Catholic population. This opposing force is here referred to collectively (and at the risk of simplification) as the 'popular' or 'liberal' side. Its component elements ranged from the *cosmhuintir* or 'lower orders' – propertyless, landless and voteless – upwards through freeholder voters (mostly mid-rank farmers, urban traders and some professionals), to the emerging priest-leaders at the top.[1] Such simple divisions mask, of course, the finer shades in between – liberal Protestants, 'Catholic Tories', and non-political priests. But the time bred polarization as the 'popular' side pushed for fundamental political change, while the Protestant ascendancy, smarting under the reforming tendencies of the Whig administration and its recent Lichfield House 'alliance' with Daniel O'Connell, bitterly resented anything – particularly intervention from the central administration in Dublin – that threatened to upset existing local power structures.

Fr Walsh's death added to the headaches of the central administration, already caught between local elite traditionalism and the forces of reform. By the mid-1830s Dublin Castle was becoming accustomed to dealing with the fallout from the murder of Protestant clergymen and the killing of police by tithe protestors (and *vice versa*), but the alleged murder of a Catholic priest by Protestants was a relatively new scenario. Under the influence of the Whig administration and of the reforming Under-Secretary, Thomas Drummond, the Castle was at great pains to act as impartially as possible in handling all these local sectarian and party controversies. Thus, in dealing with Walsh's death, the Law Adviser and Solicitor General were scrupulously impartial in their approach. In this they were supported by a number of centrally appointed officials at local level – the local stipendary magistrates, Walter Moloney, the Deputy Lieutenant of the County, Walter Blackeney, and the Inspector General of Police, Sir John Harvey, who proved equally measured in approaching the affair, and there were constant exchanges of correspondence between Dublin and Carlow as to how to deal with this most combustible of situations.

THE INQUEST

The first problem facing the Dublin administrators was whether to accept the popular version of events, that is, that a murder had occurred at Kilgraney, or, opt for the Protestant version that Walsh's death was the result of an accident. Whatever the decision, it was guaranteed to earn the Castle the odium of one party or the other, and their headaches began on the very day the body was found, with the inquest on Walsh's death. This inquest, carried out about nine hours after the body had been discovered, appeared at first sight to give a clear explanation as to how death had occurred. Two surgeons, Doctors Twomy and Fitzpatrick, were called in by the coroner to examine the body. They concluded that the injuries to Walsh's head (a 'lacerated and contused wound' below the left ear, and an extensive fracture to the base of the skull) were commensurate with a blow from a blunt, heavy object, and could not have resulted from even a precipitate fall from a horse. Though they did concede that the bruise on the dead man's left palm might have been caused by the friction of the reins when the horse started violently, they concluded that the absence of bruises on other parts of the body – particularly those of stirrup irons on the feet – indicated that the rider had not been dragged along the ground by a bolting horse. Nor did they believe that the head wound could have been caused by a horse's kick, their experience in dealing with injuries sustained by falls at Kilkenny races suggesting that in such cases the mark of a horse shoe was left on the body.[2]

The surgeons' evidence was made particularly convincing by the fact that they had considerable experience in carrying out post-mortems. Fitzpatrick, for instance, had examined the bodies of those killed in the Carrickshock tithe affray in the neighbouring county of Kilkenny some three years previously. Moreover, much of what they concluded was supported by the evidence of non-medical witnesses at the inquest, all of whom confirmed that the ground at Kilgraney bridge bore no marks of a body being dragged by a runaway horse, that there had been no streaks of road dust on the body and no blood on the dead man's clothes, while the blood spattered on the bridge parapet seemed to have come from a height rather than nearer to ground level. Everything led to the inquest concluding that Walsh had been the victim of 'wilful murder against some person or persons unknown'.[3]

But in an atmosphere of intense party feeling, nothing was as clear as it at first appeared, and the medical evidence was no exception. The problem was, hardly surprisingly, denominationally related. The two surgeons carrying out the inquest were Catholic, and were therefore seen by local Protestants as politically partisan. Consequently, to redress the balance, the inquest was resumed three days later, and three other medical men – one Catholic (Dr Kehoe) and two Protestant (the surgeons of the 57th Regiment and the

Carlow Co. Infirmary) – were brought in to further examine the exhumed body. The conclusions again reflected party as much as medical opinion, the Catholic surgeon arguing that decomposition precluded any definitive conclusion, the two Protestants claiming that Walsh's injuries were commensurate with his being thrown from a horse.[4] But the verdict of 'wilful murder' was problematic in other ways. Firstly, it had been arrived at by an inquest jury summoned not from the customary jury list provided by the baronial constable, but from a list of names given by the local Catholic clergy to the coroner – all, according to the Protestant interest in the area, qualified to act as jurors but in political terms 'most violently prejudiced men'.[5] Secondly, and more important in the opinion of Carlow conservatives, was the fact that the inquest had been attended by a large body of Catholic clergy as well as clerical students from Carlow College, and it was claimed that several of the priests had spoken or passed notes to those giving evidence, thereby interfering with the outcome of the inquest.[6] All in all, it was believed by most of the Protestant interest locally that the murder verdict was reached through clerical pressure, the timidity of the coroner (already unpopular with Protestants because he had failed to vote for his patron, Kavanagh, at the June election of that year), and the general belief that any other verdict would have led to a major eruption of popular violence – something that had to be avoided at all costs.

The violence had, indeed, already begun before the verdict was reached and the Castle's problems were compounded by the need to remain impartial while, at the same time, protecting vulnerable local Protestants from sectarian attacks. From early August onwards, a series of inflammatory sermons was preached by local Catholic priests, the one singled out for comment, unsurprisingly, being that of Walsh's uncle, John Walsh Senior, the parish priest of Borris. Replete with references to murdering Orangemen, the sermon was described by both a local JP and the military commander at Borris as 'a most violent and dangerous political discourse which was intended to agitate and excite the feelings of the populace'.[7] But popular sectarianism was only aggravated, not created, by such sermons. While Walsh's body was still lying at Kilgraney, Protestant policemen were warned not to go near the bridge. Threatening notices were posted against businessmen with Protestant conservative sympathies – millers and maltsters like Whitney of Borris and Alexander of Leighlinbridge.[8] Individual Protestants, adults and children alike, especially those lately settled on the Beresford estate at Sliguff, were threatened and hooted along the road. Shut out from the normal economic interaction of a rural area, they had to stay away from local fairs where, if they did attend, they ran the risk of either becoming involved in party quarrels or being attacked by hostile crowds.[9] For some days after the body was found, phantoms of 1798 and 1641 were raised as the police barracks at Bagenalstown became

crowded with frightened Protestants seeking protection, so much so that a
police barracks had to be established at Sliguff and the houses of those
suspected of involvement in Walsh's death had to be protected by the police
– something that continued for at least two years after the event.[10]

THE POWER OF RUMOUR

The Walsh case, irrespective of the details of the tragedy, is a case study in the
power of rumour in pre-Famine Ireland and – for the historian – a lesson in
the undependability of sources. Almost two centuries after the event, it is still
impossible to work out precisely what happened to John Walsh. This was partly
due to time and location. Although Walsh's death occurred on the roadside
within forty yards of the nearest house, nothing was seen or heard, possibly
because there actually was no altercation but, even if there was, it happened
at a late hour when most people were indoors, and on a night of very little
moonlight. Even more important, however, was that in the context of pre-
Famine Carlow, the gathering of accurate information was impeded by the
determination on either side of the denominational and party divide to believe
– and spread – the worst about the other side.[11]

At one level it was easy enough to get information. County Carlow was
well served in terms of law enforcement with over 50 magistrates and 19 police
stations.[12] Besides, although the railway to Dublin was still only in its planning
stages and would not be completed for another 20 years, a coach service meant
that communications between local officialdom and Dublin Castle was very
efficient, most correspondence taking no more than a day to make the journey
between the two centres.[13] On the other hand, much information was second-
hand. The public, though more than willing to avail of the law in bringing
cases of assault and trespass against neighbours, could when it suited them be
very sparing in the information they gave the agents of that same law.[14] The
transmission of accurate information was also hampered by the fact that local
newspapers (the conservative *Carlow Sentinel* and the O'Connellite *Carlow
Post*) each appeared only once weekly and – more importantly – that their
highly partisan attitudes meant that two contradictory stories circulated on
most issues and events. For instance, when the liberal side complained to the
Castle regarding alleged Orange provocation of locals at Graigue bridge during
the election of June 1835, the memorial was signed by 46 freeholders who
described themselves as 'hav[ing] heard and believed' details of the incident.
Even the magistrate whose report accompanied this memorial had to explain
that although he had 'heard of' the Orange incident and had 'heard of' some
conservatives carrying weapons, he had been so taken up with keeping order
in the town that he had not been able to witness personally any of these

incidents at Graigue – less than a mile distant from where he was but with the access route clogged by heaving crowds.[15]

With access to precise information so difficult, it was inevitable that Walsh's death would spawn all sorts of stories. Hardly had the body been discovered than the news began to spread that the priest had most certainly been murdered. Excitement spiralled as local people objected to the removal of the corpse until it could be examined by doctors who could confirm their suspicions.[16] Within three days of the tragedy, rumour had become fact, print media and the popular sung grapevine of the ballad singers combining to spread the story. Broadside ballads, produced by local jobbing printers and sung around town and county, called for 'a curse on those bloody murderers who took [Walsh's] life away', while the listening crowds called for the Orangemen to be turned out of town.[17] The story soon spread beyond the circuit of jobbing printers and plebeian minstrels. The *Freeman's Journal* headlined its first report of the priest's death with the words 'Orange Barbarity' and nine months later was still describing what had happened as murder.[18] Confused rumours proliferated regarding the weapon – if murder there was. The story spread, based on the first report of the affair in the *Freeman's Journal*, that Walsh had been killed by a gunshot – a belief apparently deriving in turn from another priest's account of shots being fired in the vicinity of Kilgraney bridge a fortnight before, a story taken up within a week by some London papers.[19] Even when the inquest concluded that death had been caused, not by a gunshot but by a blow from a blunt instrument, hypothesis again became reality and a local stonemason employed by Archibald Sly received anonymous threats that '[we will] make four quarters of yourself and your wife and family', on the grounds that he had deliberately left his mason's hammer lying around for the killers to use on Walsh.[20]

One sequence of spurious evidence bred another – spread by word of mouth and through posters, scrawled notices and the partisan and frequently inaccurate reports in newspaper columns. When Anne Rooney, one of the first to give information in the Walsh case (probably false, as things turned out) made her way from Naas south to Carlow in the early days of August 1835, the news of the priest's death must have reached her through conversations along the way (she was illiterate, so the printed or written word, if she saw it, must have had to be mediated for her). She, having heard and expanded on the story of Sly's complicity in the murder of Walsh, became in her turn the object of further rumour. When the inconsistency of her evidence became apparent, and she was arrested for perjury, she was locked out of her lodgings and crowds gathered to attack her, not because she had spread false information but because the word had travelled that she had been 'bought over' by the authorities, and she had to be kept hidden in the courthouse until darkness fell and she could be brought safely to new accommodation.[21] Gradually the tissue of tales became even more tangled when recent events merged with religious beliefs (or superstition, depending on the point of view): people arrived at Kilgraney bridge to dip their handkerchiefs into the blood of a martyr, and over the following months people knelt and prayed at the spot where the body had been found, while talk of miraculous cures also spread.[22]

This conversion of fiction into fact was not confined to the popular side. The Protestant conservative version of events also rested heavily on hearsay. A local police constable, revealing his own party credentials by referring to the dead man as 'Priest Walsh', reported to the Castle that Walsh's death was *definitely* due to a fall from his horse, while the local conservative *Carlow Sentinel* added that Walsh had been drunk when the accident occurred, assuming that it was he, and not his travelling companion Fr James Nolan, that had attended the 'convivial party' at Clogrenan.[23] The 'starting horse' figured prominently in these rumours. While Nolan's evidence at Sly's trial the following March indicated that he was only vaguely aware that the horse had once thrown Walsh, the *Sentinel*'s report of the inquest described Nolan's account quite differently: 'This horse had thrown Mr Walsh at different times, that he himself had advised him to part with the animal, and that on the very night of his death he begged of Mr Walsh not to attempt to ride him home.'[24]

Stories on this, as on the popular side, reflected and fed on a combination of stereotypes, facts and rumour. The extreme Protestant view of Catholic priests, particularly Irish Catholic priests, as a drunken and conniving lot, became mixed with the reality that Walsh had socialized with some other priests on the night of his death. The conservative press initiated its own wildfire spread of the drunken Walsh story, reproducing the *Dublin Evening Post's* wink-wink reference to 'the after-dinner habits of the popish priests', an insinuation that then found its way back into the columns of the local *Carlow Sentinel*.[25] Nor were provincial borders a barrier to the spread of rumour. Within a few days of Walsh's death and for months thereafter, the contradictory versions of the story were being published in the press far and wide – throughout Ireland, in Britain, and even as far afield as the United States, the London *Times*, in particular, continuing to keep an eye on the fall-out from the event over the following five years.[26]

3. Procuring evidence

Rumour abounded but there was little evidence. Why? The 'Protestant answer' was that where there had been no murder there could be no evidence – a viewpoint that is temptingly attractive even for a historian at the remove of two centuries, especially since most of the evidence that did emerge was offered a very long time – up to six months – after the priest's death. The 'popular answer' was more complicated, justifying witnesses' reticence and delay in coming forward in a number of ways. Some who did eventually testify had been employed by the suspects or the state and did not want to risk their wages until their term in service had finished or until their consciences finally pushed them to tell their stories.[1] Others apparently feared to give information lest they be turned out of their holdings, particularly if they held without a lease. One landless man, Matthew Murphy, who gave his statement six months after Walsh's death, explained his reticence thus 'He has been obliged to live with a brother's son at Ballinkillen, who holds a small farm under Lord Beresford, and that he was unwilling to say much, lest it might injure his nephew who has not got a lease on his farm'.[2] While this fear was probably greatly exaggerated, it was not as farfetched as at first appears. Eviction as a punishment for troublesome tenants was not unknown. The *Carlow Sentinel* on more than one occasion recommended it as a punishment for tenants who had voted against their landlords, and the townland of Sliguff had already seen politically motivated evictions by Lord Beresford four years previously while similar measures were threatened following the election of June 1835.[3] The Bruen estate records, too, show that following the June election detailed notes were made of the name, valuation, religion and voting record of every tenant on the poll book, with accompanying comments on the action to be taken regarding the tenure of those who had voted against the conservative candidates, one of whom was Bruen himself.[4] With all these considerations in mind, individuals might well think twice before testifying, even – or perhaps especially – in the case of the alleged murder of a priest by a local Protestant.

But even without direct witnesses, a great deal of vague and intriguing information floated around in the immediate aftermath of the priest's death. A number of people living in the environs of Kilgraney recounted how on the night of Walsh's death they had seen Archibald Sly riding along the road at Cloughwater in the general vicinity of the bridge, a suspicious matter since the spot where he was seen was nearly six miles from his own residence at

Sliguff and was not on his normal route home *via* Ballinkillin.[5] Other
mutterings suggested that local Protestants, if not actually implicated in murder,
had been planning something against Walsh. At the inquest one particularly
credible witness, a man known for avoiding party entanglements, claimed that
he had met a group of eight men at Kilgraney bridge about two hours before
Walsh's death, three of whom had come from 'the new range of building' (that
is, the farmhouses in course of construction for Protestant tenants) and that
when they recognized him they mumbled something 'as if disappointed'.[6]
Other witnesses gave an account of the knowing comments passed by one of
the three suspects as the crowd began to gather the next morning around the
dead body. Abraham Wynne, who seemed tipsy, had declared that 'many people
were talking and bladdering about this who knew nothing at all about it, but
that there were some people not far off who could tell a good deal about it if
they wished'.[7]

Over the following days, more evidence trickled in, but its value was
negligible in view of the seriously delusional or even suicidal tendencies of
the witnesses. One man named John Brown handed himself up to the police
in Athy, claiming that he himself had killed Walsh, but on appearing at the
Carlow petty sessions, admitted that he had nothing at all to do with the
matter. It soon transpired that he was an unemployed teacher who had recently
'lost' (his own words) his wife and children, though in what circumstances
was not clear. The poor man seems to have hoped that if convicted of Walsh's
murder he would be executed and thus terminate a life of misery, but he
withdrew his story when 'the thought flashed across his mind that it would
be equally culpable to come by his death [through hanging] as if he committed
suicide' and the case was dismissed.[8]

A further dramatic story came from a Carlow shoemaker, named Brooder
or Broderick, who claimed to have helped two strange men to kill Walsh, but
his evidence, too, proved useless when he mistakenly identified the brother of
a local priest as one of the two.[9] The magistrates who took his statement did
not believe a word he uttered, but found themselves caught in a not
uncommon dilemma between common sense, the law and public opinion. As
one of them expressed it,

> I have not the slightest hesitation in saying that I do not credit one word
> of [Broderick's statement], yet from the excitement which exists, if we
> refused to listen to him without a reference to the Government, it might
> hereafter be said that … where an approver had offered, we had rejected
> him … I think the man ought to be committed on his own confession
> as an accessory in the murder, and yet I don't see how we can well do
> that, when we do not credit his statement …

The headaches caused to the authorities by such an unreliable witness were finally dispelled when Broderick confessed that the entire story was a fiction, concocted by him when he was drunk.[10] It was this lack of direct evidence along with the Castle's presumed tardiness in tackling the problem that led, two weeks after Walsh's death, to the offer by the Catholic clergy and leading freeholders of the county of a reward of £600 for information leading to the apprehension of the killer.[11] The offer of a reward was successful in unleashing a flow of information so suddenly that it led to claims (hardly unwarranted) by Sly's supporters that 'evidence' was being concocted for the purpose of financial gain and also with the added bonus in the popular mind that such evidence would prove the undoing of a local Protestant. At the court cases following the death, every witness against Sly or in favour of his accusers was questioned in some way on the role the announcement of the reward had played in his or her coming forward.[12]

The most dramatic information came from Anne Rooney, the previously mentioned young female servant of no fixed abode, who happened to be passing through Co. Carlow in mid-August 1835. In her evidence, presented to the magistrate three weeks after Walsh's death, she claimed that she had actually witnessed Sly, Styles and Wynne attack Walsh with a crowbar and a hammer, while she and two other women hid behind some bushes nearby.[13] Two months later, the second major piece of evidence against Sly came from James Doyle, a 21-year-old farm servant who had worked for Sly for almost a year.[14] He claimed that while he feigned sleep in the settle bed in Sly's kitchen on the night of the murder, he heard Sly describe the murder to two late night callers who worked on the Kavanagh estate, and one of whom was Sly's nephew: 'I caught Walsh's reins, and he made a blow at me, his horse started, and I got a blow of his whip. Wynne then knocked him down and Styles leaped on him and we finished him'.[15] Doyle's evidence was corroborated by another of Sly's workmen, the 15-year-old Patrick Fleming, who had been sleeping in the kitchen on the same occasion, and who alleged that he also had heard the discussion about 'knocking down blind Jack Walsh'.[16] The third separate significant piece of information came from a Catholic policeman, Hugh Corrigan, who gave a similar account of how, when he was on duty protecting Sly's house from popular attack some days after Walsh's death, he had overheard a conversation in which Sly's uncle berated him for his involvement in the attack: 'Archy, you're a foolish man to have anything to do in this business, for so sure as Aby Wynne is taken … he will inform against you all and ye will be hanged, every man'.[17]

In spite, or perhaps because, of the dramatic nature of these three separate stories, there were serious flaws in each. Anne Rooney's account, one of the few based on apparent first-hand evidence, was quickly discredited when the women she said had witnessed the killing along with her, denied all knowledge

of both the incident and of Rooney herself. Her evidence was further
undermined when the cousins she claimed to have in Carlow town could not
be found, and when word arrived that on the very night she claimed to have
seen Walsh murdered, Rooney had actually been in Naas jail serving a three-
month sentence for larceny.[18] Not surprisingly, her evidence was dismissed,
and she was held over to be tried for perjury at the following assizes.[19]

The accounts that came from the two workmen, Doyle and Fleming, and
from the policeman, Corrigan, initially appeared much more credible than that
of Rooney, and local magistrates took great care that their statements were
carefully recorded and sent to Dublin for perusal by the Law Advisor, Crown
Solicitor and Attorney General.[20] But there were several attendant problems.
Firstly, some apparently watertight points were easily disputed by the defence.
This was the case with the bruise on Sly's forehead which was first noticed
on the day after Walsh's death. All witnesses, both pro- and anti-Sly, agreed
that the bruise was newly acquired. But whereas the stories of Doyle and
Fleming put it as acquired in the struggle with Walsh, Sly claimed, quite
credibly, that it was the result of his knocking into a branch 'going up to Mr
Kavanagh's'.[21] Secondly, even if the stories incriminating Sly were true, it would
prove very difficult to convict him. The reason was that the three accounts were
based not on eye-witness accounts but on reports of overheard conversations in
which, despite Sly implicating himself in the killing of Walsh, he had stated that
it was actually Wynne that had struck the fatal blow – 'Wynne is the man that
used the hammer and killed him'.[22] Therefore, while this was a joint attack where
'the blow of any one individual is the blow of all', Sly might be exonerated by
the very words that the witnesses intended to incriminate him, and he was
unlikely to act at his own trial as a witness against the two other suspects.[23]

The other and more obvious problem was that the three men's evidence
against Sly might prove to be a complete fiction. As the counsel for the defence
pointed out at Sly's trial, it was unlikely that murderers fresh from the scene
of crime would have discussed their deeds in a place where they were likely
to be overheard, especially since Sly's house contained three other rooms where
such matters might have been discussed in private. On the other hand, such
indiscretion was entirely possible, at least on Sly's part, since he seems (as will
be discussed later) to have been something of an irascible character. More
importantly, he seems to have been labouring under the effects of alcohol both
on the night Walsh died and on later occasions when, witnesses claimed, his
references to his role in Walsh's death were made when he was 'purty hearty'.[24]

Even more problematic were the combined discrepancies and suspicious
consistencies between the different pieces of evidence and between the
successive statements given by each separate witness. Fleming described Sly's
conversation as being held with two policemen rather than with his nephew
and the Kavanagh estate employee, though whether this was a piece of fiction

or the mistaken telescoping of two separate incidents is impossible to decide. Corrigan's story was even more unbelievable. He testified not only to hearing the incriminating conversation between Sly and his uncle, but also to having seen Sly riding at a 'hard gallop' near Sliguff between eleven and twelve on the night of Walsh's death. The barracks duty books, however, showed that Corrigan had arrived back indoors at eleven. Though his claim that this was an inaccurate entry by his sergeant, Francis Patterson (and he may well have been right in this as there were hints of tension between them), his failure to bring this up for two months after making his initial statement cast doubts on the validity of his entire story.[25] Moreover, the wording of his evidence in court was almost verbatim with his original statement before the magistrates four months previously, and the same was evident in the case of Doyle. Was this striking consistency an indication of the accuracy of the evidence? Was it due to constant rehearsal by honest individuals conscious that they could be outsmarted in the witness box by the lawyers for the defence? Or, as the trial judge (and, eventually, the jury also) concluded, was it a sign that the stories were rote-learned fictions: 'All I have to say is, my man, I envy your memory!' – a comment that quickly translated into a conviction for perjury.[26]

There is no doubt that much of the evidence against Sly was extremely problematic, but for those seeking his conviction, the difficulties were compounded by the fact that the witnesses were individuals of very little account socially. While the reforming state of the 1830s subscribed to the belief that all were equal before the law, there was no doubt that the social status and public reputation of an individual could affect his or her credibility in the eyes of a jury. This was clear in the reaction to the witnesses at the inquest immediately after Walsh's death. Well over half those giving evidence were collier workers, labourers, smallholders and landless individuals whose lack of a 'stake' in society meant that their evidence was treated with some suspicion by contemporary commentators. This was largely because they were considered to be easy dupes of more manipulative individuals, and in the highly charged sectarian atmosphere of pre-Famine Carlow the string pullers were assumed to be the priests. Other witnesses – doctors, Catholic priests and one substantial farmer – were considered more reliable, and though their creed and party alignment was considered (not incorrectly) to colour their evidence, there was less derision poured on the accounts they gave.[27] This emphasis on the character and track record of the witnesses was to prove particularly important in the lead-up to Sly's trial. The testimony of Anne Rooney, even before her perjury was proven, was regarded with particular suspicion by the local magistrates on the grounds that she was a 'most abandoned creature' – an accurate enough assessment, as events proved.[28] And yet, despite the apparently conclusive proof that Rooney had been far away from Kilgraney on the night she claimed to have witnessed the murder of Walsh, her exchanges at her trial

at the next assizes, especially with those whom she had called as her alibis –
'They are all denying me now, so they are' – leave one with the feeling that
there were some grains of truth in her story and that she was as conscious
then as is today's researcher that her word would never be believed because
she was a vagrant.[29]

The social position of the two servant boys and the policeman was
considerably more respectable than that of Rooney, but their credibility as
witnesses was compromised by aspects of their own pasts. Doyle had been
reputedly dismissed by Sly for 'night walking' – that is, staying out late and
keeping bad company – while Corrigan had served a spell in prison, though
when and for what was never explained.[30] Possibly most damaging for
Corrigan was the way in which discrepancies in his evidence meshed with a
record of apparent insubordination while in the service. He had fallen foul of
his sergeant, Francis Patterson – when is not clear – for disobeying an order
to deliver a letter into Carlow, and Patterson, who did not force the issue –
again for reasons that remain a mystery – was later dismissed for neglect of
duty.[31] Corrigan's claim that the entry of his return to barracks on the night
of 30 July had been falsified by Patterson gained no credence in court. In fact,
it was one of the many points that convinced the jury that Corrigan was lying.
Neither was there any mention at Sly's trial of Patterson's dismissal from the
constabulary, though this had occurred four months earlier. Had Sly's defence
wished to use it (as both the conservative press and Carlow's Protestant
magistrates saw it) as proof that the government had loaded the dice unfairly
against Sly and all upholders of the law, then it surely should have been brought
up in court. Had Patterson, therefore, been aligned with the conservative
interest in Carlow? Patrick Fleming's evidence (extremely garbled and not
very credible) mentioned Sly boasting to two policemen (Michael Hoey and
someone whose first name was George) about how he had 'knocked down
little blind Jack Walsh', and though Patterson's name was not mentioned, four
years later it was alleged that he had actually spent a night in Sly's company
and that this was the real reason for his dismissal from the force.[32] Again, the
mesh of conflicting evidence, lies and half-told stories makes it impossible to
decide whether the anti-Sly evidence was undermined by a deliberate smear
campaign on the part of the local conservative interest, or whether the
witnesses were – as the courts eventually decided – perjuring themselves to
destroy Sly and to claim the £600 reward.

PIG IN THE MIDDLE

The state and its local representatives, caught between contending parties, had
the thankless task of trying to balance irreconcilable evidence and to ensure

justice in a situation where both sides loudly accused it of partiality. Disgruntled conservatives in Carlow and beyond saw the Castle and its local representatives as excessively receptive to the claim that Walsh had been murdered. They were particularly riled that Archibald Sly, insult added to injury by his arrest on the evidence of his own servant boys and a Catholic policeman, was refused bail, despite the considerable efforts on his behalf by his attorney and the local Protestant elite.[33] Nor was the popular side happy with the Dublin administration. Though the stipendary magistrates and the priests had cooperated closely in keeping the peace during the June 1835 election (something which infuriated local conservatives), these same priests now claimed that Dublin was tardy in initiating a thorough investigation into the Walsh case. The Castle's failure to offer a reward for the apprehension of the killer (an indication of Dublin's doubts regarding the murder claim) became a major bone of contention. Indeed, the organizing of the reward (involving over 400 contributions ranging from 5s. upwards to £10) and its publication through both Sunday sermons and printed posters, became in itself an expression of popular solidarity in the face of both conservative hostility and perceived government apathy.[34]

The difficulty of presiding over a divided society was made clear in the months preceding and following Walsh's death when the Castle was barraged from both sides of the Carlow party divide. In June 1835 two opposing memorials arrived in quick succession in relation to the confrontation at Graigue during the June election. One memorial from the popular side, headed by the redoubtable James Maher, parish priest of Carlow and administrator of the diocese, decried Orange arrogance, while the other from a group of Queen's Co. magistrates, led by Barker Thacker, treasurer of the Grand Lodge of Queen's Co., complained of mob rule.[35] Two months later, Walsh's death was the signal for another paper war. First, a memorial arrived in Dublin from Carlow Protestants who complained, not without reason, about the entirely Catholic character of the inquest jury, the poster announcing the reward for information about the murderer following on its heels.[36] Another three months on, the allegedly provocative behaviour of two locally stationed army regiments brought on more competing memorials; one from the local liberals headed by James Maher called for a public enquiry into the soldiers' behaviour, to be followed closely by another from the Protestant inhabitants and magistrates of Carlow (though with a few liberals also signing) in support of the army.[37] In March 1836 yet another memorial was sent to the Castle, this time from the Protestant magistrates who supported the (possibly Protestant) police sergeant, Francis Patterson, against his dismissal for neglect of his duty, to be followed later in the year by a memorial from the other side regarding the allegedly provocative activities of local Orangemen in Kiledmond between Borris and the Wexford border.[38]

THE JURY ISSUE

Trapped in this unenviable position as 'pig in the middle', the Dublin administration went to considerable lengths to be fair, and be *seen to be so*, in dealing with the Walsh affair. The acceptance of the Carlow inquest jury's murder verdict, the admission as evidence of the statements of Doyle, Fleming and Corrigan, and the refusal to admit Sly to bail, had put the Castle (at least in the eyes of disgruntled conservatives) firmly on the popular side. Once the court case loomed, however, the anxiety to regain the middle ground, combined with a genuine wish to see justice done, made the Castle lean quite perceptibly towards Sly's side. A month before the trial, his attorney was given all the relevant documentation, including the witnesses' statements, enabling him to call for the witnesses most likely to support his case.[39] He was, moreover, particularly advantaged by the way the state dealt with the calling of the trial jury. It was legally accepted that, in the interests of a fair trial, both prosecutor and defendant had the right of 'peremptory challenge', that is, they could reject up to 20 jurors without stating the reason.[40] Sly, through his attorney, challenged nine jurors in this way, without stating why but clearly on the grounds of their party and religious bias, and his challenges were accepted by the trial judge.[41] The prosecution, on the other hand, eager to make the state's impartiality as clearly visible as possible, followed to the letter the new legislation that had prohibited the rejection of jurors on the grounds of either religion or party, and it challenged no juror whatever. As the Crown Solicitor observed later, Sly's object was 'to have a jury composed exclusively of Protestants', and the result was precisely that – one member was a 'conservative Roman Catholic', while the other 11 were Protestant conservatives 'with strong political feelings'.[42]

'Implicit in every discussion of 19th-century Irish juries was the belief that either the sheriff or the Crown Solicitor had packed them'.[43] In the case of Sly's trial, most balanced observers agreed that his acquittal was in reality due not to jury manipulation but to the court's rightful rejection of perjured evidence – even the *Freeman's Journal* having no apparent quarrel with the verdict. But there was a frisson of unease about the general operation of the trial.[44] Liberals, though agreeing that no other verdict *could* have been reached in view of the evidence available, were convinced that what had actually triumphed was party, and that the law had been used to ensure this result. Conservatives were elated, since it was on the very same issue of the composition of the jury that the murder verdict had been reached at the inquest on Walsh's body seven months previously, but their delight only served to convince the popular side that justice had been denied.

If the Dublin administration had hoped the controversy would end there, it was to be disappointed.[45] As soon as Sly pressed for the arrest of Doyle,

Fleming and Corrigan for perjury, the Castle was in another bind.[46] Legal considerations apart, political expediency demanded that Protestant opinion continue to be placated by bringing the three witnesses to trial. The matter was rendered more urgent by the mislaying of one of the files from the original trial – a matter portrayed by the *Carlow Sentinel* and its supporters as a deliberate attempt to rig matters in favour of the Walsh camp.[47] In fact, the problem was solved by the Castle's producing a set of duplicate notes, taken at Sly's trial by a government shorthand notetaker brought to Carlow expressly for this purpose, but this did little to persuade Sly's supporters of the impartiality of the central administration. Nor, unsurprisingly, did the ensuing conviction of the three witnesses for perjury win the Castle any support on the popular side, where the belief spread that the legal system had been stage-managed again in favour of the conservative interest. This belief was enforced by the clearly hostile attitude of the trial judge, Baron Smith, towards the anti-Sly witnesses, and by the fact that it was the foreman of the jury (a leading Carlow conservative, Henry Newton) who, once Sly had been acquitted, called for the arrest of the discredited witnesses.[48] Again, the debate centred not so much on whether perjury had been committed by Doyle, Fleming and Corrigan – most observers seem to have accepted that it had – but on the manner of calling a jury. It was claimed by the liberals, through their spokesman Fr James Maher, that the juries in all three cases were deliberately tailored so as to secure a conviction. In Corrigan's case, the setting aside of three Catholics who had been struck off the voting registry for insufficient qualification was the first measure taken to disadvantage the accused, with the result that there was only one Catholic on the jury. In Doyle's trial, it was claimed that six Catholic jurors present when the Clerk of the Court made the first call, had been passed over in favour of Protestant jurors arriving in time for the second call, thus ensuring a Protestant majority on that jury, too. Genuinely anxious that there had been irregularities, the Castle immediately demanded an explanation from the Clerk of the Court. His assurance that the Catholic jurors had not actually answered the first call was accepted by the Castle but at popular level the information that the law had been obeyed to the letter did nothing to dispel the suspicion that party bias, even if it had not actually determined the outcome of the trials, did determine the *manner* in which that outcome was reached.[49]

4. Great hatred, little room

The party animosity manifest in the trials following the death of Walsh was not in the least unusual in the Ireland of 1835, but its articulation in the Carlow context was particularly vindictive.[1] Was this because the narrowness of this local arena – Carlow is the second smallest county on the island, with an area of a little over 221,000 acres – condensed and intensified animosities?[2] Impartial observers – and there were few of these apart from the stipendary magistrates and the Inspector General of Police – confirmed this when they claimed that the controversy would have fizzled out much sooner had it not been fanned into a flame by locally produced provocative ballads, sermons and newspaper articles.[3]

There is no doubt that Carlow's traditional elite (mostly, though not entirely, Protestant) was spoiling for a fight in the mid-1830s. It was particularly resentful of what it saw as Dublin Castle's tampering with the magistracy and, since the mid-1820s had resisted the appointment of stipendary magistrates who worked alongside, but sometimes counter to, the local Justices of the Peace. This antipathy was partly due to the expense of the stipendary system, but more so to the capacity of the new appointments to disturb traditional networks of patronage and authority.[4] The main bone of contention was the maintenance of law and order – a matter of much importance in the heady atmosphere of the 1830s. The stipendary magistrates, under instructions from Dublin Castle, made considerable efforts to strike a balance between control and persuasion when dealing with volatile crowds on the one hand and, unwisely assertive members of the elite on the other.[5] Such conciliatory tactics were despised by the local elite. They much preferred the no-nonsense approach of the Justices of the Peace who, drawn from among the local gentry and landed interest, were more in harmony with traditional thinking about the maintenance of public order. When the popular *Leinster Independent* described them as 'Orange magistrates', it was guilty of overstatement, but its assertion was revealing in two ways. Firstly, it rightly stressed the old magistrates' partisan character and their capacity to exacerbate public disorder through their inflexible outlook and their preference for crowd control 'in the old usual way – at the point of a bayonet'.[6] Secondly, it reflected the thinking of the increasingly prosperous and politically conscious Catholic middle class – publicans, grocers, pig dealers, pawnbrokers and professionals – in Carlow, Tullow, Bagenalstown and Borris, whose aspirations, both social and political, were given voice by an increasingly vocal Catholic clergy.[7] Since the late 1820s these were active in a local Liberal Club that had built up popular electoral strength and scrutinized the actions of the magistracy – a double brief that made them obnoxious to the old elite, who mercilessly ridiculed their plebeian ancestry but who were fearful of their capacity to undermine traditional institutions.[8]

In Carlow, however, despite the undoubted assertiveness of this rising middle class, the political agenda was largely dominated by land-related rather than urban issues. This was due both to the smallness of the middle class, and to the blurring of the line between urban and rural in a county where the prosperity of towns was inextricably linked with the fortunes of agriculture. For example, some landed proprietors like John Alexander of Sliguff also ran mills and warehouses in Carlow and Leighlinbridge, while millers like Samuel Crosthwait owned concerns in both Carlow and Bagenalstown.[9] Politically, too, county and town merged into each other, families dominating the county representation also playing a role in that of the borough, while the elections for both county and borough members took place in the county town of Carlow. This compactness bred introversion, especially within the leaderships on both sides of the political and denominational divide. Landed proprietors socialized together, intermarried and were active in various associational bodies ranging from agricultural societies to the London Missionary Society, while the Catholic clergy, as clear from the activities of John Walsh on the day of his death, had their own increasingly introverted social network.[10] This same compactness in turn bred inter-group tension as a small number of rivals, some long established, some *parvenu*, battled it out for control of the same small county.

In another way, it was Carlow's tendency to look outwards that intensified party tensions. County boundaries, while important administratively, were in many ways artificial. Not only did the physical and economic landscapes ignore such divisions, but so did other administrative and economic units. Catholic and Established Church parishes stretched into different counties, the Catholic parish of Borris, for example, covered parts of several civil parishes and stretched into Co. Kilkenny while the civil parish similarly crossed county boundaries. Landed estates like those of Lord Courtown were scattered through a number of counties, while a sizeable proportion of Carlow's parliamentary voters were resident in Queen's Co. and Kildare. For agrarian movements like the Rockites of the 1820s and the Whitefeet of the early 1830s county boundaries were much less relevant than shared terrain, while at a different social level, the management styles of landlords and their agents were informed by their experience in other counties, frequently far from Carlow.[11] The links with other counties ensured that Carlow was closely affected by political events elsewhere. Incidents like the tithe-related Carrickshock affair that had occurred in south Kilkenny in late 1831 coloured the popular imagination in Carlow for a considerable time, the barony of Rathvilly, for instance resounding to calls of 'Carrickshock!' when attempts were made to collect tithe locally in mid-1834.[12] Above the level of the *cosmhuintir*, awareness of developments beyond the county bounds was fostered by the local newspapers. Both the conservative *Carlow Sentinel* and the reformist *Leinster Independent* circulated in five counties – Carlow itself, Queen's, Kildare, Wicklow and Wexford – and carried their news and that of Kilkenny, whose own newspapers in turn covered events in Carlow.

It was from the late 1820s onwards, in Carlow as in neighbouring counties, that the party race for local control accelerated. Simultaneously encouraged by state reform and resentful that the pace was not fast enough, popular agitation snowballed against multiple aspects of the old regime. A major flashpoint in this clash of worlds was in the south Leinster area – Queen's Co., Kilkenny, Wexford and Carlow – where the anti-tithe campaign led to a wave of popular agitation involving public meetings, communal resistance to the serving of tithe notices, boycotting of auctions of confiscated animals, and the introduction of the tithe issue into parliamentary elections.[13] Equally indicative of the struggle between the old and the new was the growing challenge to the landed ascendancy's hold on parliamentary representation by (sometimes nominally) liberal candidates who took up Daniel O'Connell's calls for reform and repeal of the Union. From the early 1830s onwards, a number of fiercely contested elections took place in Carlow – elections that showed not just how strongly landlord political control was challenged but also how determinedly the landlords fought that challenge.[14]

PARLIAMENTARY REPRESENTATION

Since the Union, Carlow county had two parliamentary representatives, the seats passing between a number of families – Burtons, Burghs, Butlers, La Touches and others. By the 1830s the representation was dominated by two major landed families from the south of the county, the Kavanaghs of Borris and the Bruens of Oak Park, the latter family continuing to represent the county until the 1880s.[15] While elections were generally uncontested for the first 30 years of the 19th century, the reform act of 1832 launched a struggle for the control of the constituency. In a county where even the post-reform electorate amounted to less than 2% of the population, the continuing family control of the county representation depended on landlords' ability to manage the votes of the enfranchised tenants on their estates.[16]

In this they came into direct conflict with politically active priests who asserted that 'the right of the landlord to the suffrage of the tenant ... has long passed away among the other feudal rights'.[17] John Walsh of Borris was one

such priest, involved in politics since his arrival in Borris parish in the mid-
1820s.[18] Though he did not take the lead role in mobilizing the voters (it was
his uncle, as parish priest, who always spoke first at meetings and who led the
voters into the poll in Carlow) he seems to have been extremely vocal in
expressing his political opinions, especially regarding local conservative
landlords. The protagonists faced each other down at the registries and at
election time but the struggle was an ongoing one, informing the rhetoric and
outlook of both sides as each claimed an authority based on superior antiquity.
The 'priests' party' as the local magistrate, Robert Doyne described it, attacked
the conservative landed proprietors as *parvenus* – 'fellows whose names were
not known when [the people's] ancestors possessed the land they now claim'.[19]
The conservative side responded in kind. At meetings of agricultural societies
and at entertainments thrown for estate workers, the common interests of
landlord and tenant formed a major theme, and landlords' communications
with tenants stressed that priests were 'false friends who only seek to serve
their own purposes, and who are as unwilling as they are unable to stand by
you when friendship requires proof'.[20]

The priests' dismissal of the landed elite as 'Johnnies-come-lately' was met
with counter claims of antiquity. John Ryan, one of the county's leading
Orangemen, in compiling his *History and antiquities of the county of Carlow* in
the early 1830s, included a long section on the (largely Protestant) historic
families of the region.[21] In similar vein, as the sitting MPs for the county faced
a growing electoral challenge in 1834, the *Carlow Sentinel* resurrected and
published a testimonial that had been presented to Bruen's father forty years
previously in 1795 in recognition of his 'princely munificence, his unbounded
hospitality, and above all, the noble qualities with which he was endowed'. A
year later, in celebration of the conservative victory in the January election,
the same paper published a glowing description of a victory celebration at
Borris House, a short distance from the residence of the Fathers Walsh, rubbing
salt into clerical wounds by comparing Kavanagh to 'the feudal barons or
chieftains of old, surrounded by his hardy clansmen and dependants'.[22]

In this race between landed interest and priest-led popular side, the control
of electoral registration became particularly important. No sooner had the 40s.
freeholders been disfranchised under the terms of Emancipation in 1829 than
both landlords and priests competed to re-register former 40s. freeholders as
£10 freeholders – a venture involving maximal equivocation and minimal
scrupulosity. This practice continued into the 1830s, valuations being inflated
(or deflated) as the need of the rival parties demanded. Some townlands were
particularly targeted for such inflated valuation – Roscat near Tullow (with
no one strong landlord to prevent subdivision) achieving a notoriety in this
regard – while the hapless tenant found himself caught between the two
protagonists.[23] It was hardly surprising that many tenants, whose acreage and

valuation entitled them to vote, proved less than enthusiastic about claiming and exercising a right that would make them 'either quarrel with the clergyman or quarrel with their landlord' each capable of ruthlessly punishing non-compliance.[24] Faced with the prospect of spiritual penalties and popular odium on the one hand, and eviction or being pressed for overdue rent on the other, at least some farmers did their very best to avoid the dubious privilege of the vote. They either declined the offer of a lease, even where a lease would bring added economic security, or did their utmost to dodge being (as the admittedly biased *Carlow Sentinel* expressed it) 'dragged forward to register'.[25] Once registered, escape was impossible. The voter was visited by his landlord or the landlord's supporters, who reminded him to vote the right way, or by the priest, or – even more frightening – by crowds of non-voters, who threatened dire consequences for non-compliance. This was what faced John Byrne of Harroldstown in the barony of Rathvilly in January 1835, when a mob of between three and four hundred persons converged on his house, warning him not to vote for Bruen.[26] On the morning of the election, those who had openly committed themselves to the popular side marched into Carlow headed and followed by their priests, while those who had opted for the landlord side drove into town in the transport supplied by the gentry. The polling was equally public, but even if a secret franchise had pertained, it was almost impossible to hide one's vote from an all-too-interested public, even more so to escape the consequences that followed.

The manipulation of registration and voting, and the wild excitement produced by contested elections in an age when party passions were high and when public entertainment was minimal, led to a pendulum-like swing in election results in Carlow in the first half of the 1830s.[27] The 1832 election saw a bitter contest in which the Protestant Kavanagh and Bruen were defeated by the Catholic Walter Blackney and Thomas Wallace.[28] More mayhem followed in 1835 with two elections in quick succession. In February Kavanagh and Bruen defeated the Repealers, Maurice O'Connell and Michael Cahill, but were unseated on the grounds of undue influence. Another election was held four months later, with the same conservative candidates facing the challenge of two different O'Connell-backed candidates, Nicholas Vigors and Alexander Raphael, who were victorious by a margin of fifty-five votes. They, in their turn, were unseated when a parliamentary enquiry into dubious and contested registration practices led to over a hundred of their supporters being struck off the register on the grounds of insufficient or irregular property qualifications.[29] Bruen and Kavanagh then took the seats again, but the brief victory of the popular side struck at the very heart of landed and Protestant political control in the county, while whetting the appetites of those who sought change. The atmosphere, already tense, was soured by the triumphalism of whichever side was in the ascendant and by the absolute fury of the vanquished. Thus, the Kavanagh and Bruen victory of January 1835 was literally shoved in the faces of the defeated popular side, particularly in the town of Borris, by the illumination of Protestant houses and by the holding of a celebratory banquet at Kavanagh's residence, attended by 150 tenants and a large number of gentlemen.[30] The defeated responded in kind, crowds assaulting conservative voters whose identity had been publicized through blacklists as far away as Athy, and wreaking havoc on the property of those who had been active on the victorious side.[31] One Bagenalstown innkeeper who had voted conservative and helped to convey conservative voters to the poll now found his stable burned to the ground with the loss of the very horses that he had used to transport the voters to Carlow.[32]

The popular jubilation following the (short-lived) victory of Vigors and Raphael in the June election led to equal public disruption. Faceless popular supporters thumbed their noses at the Protestant gentry by burning fox covers and poisoning horses, especially hunters, not in any indiscriminate fashion but targeting especially those individuals like Robert Doyne, William Duckett and Thomas Watson who were prominent conservatives or unpopular magistrates.[33] The parliamentary committee established to investigate allegations of electoral corruption, far from lessening the conflict, only added to its intensity, the popular side complaining loudly that the committee's membership of eight Tories and three Liberals was weighted in favour of the Protestant side, while the conservative press gleefully published weekly reports of the progressive striking of unqualified O'Connellite voters from the electoral register.[34] It is against this immediate background of contested political space and rising popular excitement that the controversy surrounding John Walsh's death must be viewed.

POLITICAL PRIESTS

Any estimate of the role of the Catholic clergy in pre-Famine Carlow involves the balancing of deeply conflicting sources. The O'Connellite media – the *Freeman's Journal, Carlow Evening Post* and *Leinster Independent* – presented the priests as popular champions, 'the natural and able protectors of the people';[35] nor was this an inaccurate estimate. Though there was a wide social gulf between them and most of their flocks, priests were frequently the main source of charity for the destitute in the absence of a Poor Law, and they acted as intermediaries between state and local community and as publicizers of popular grievance.[36] Since the early 1830s, when they moved to the forefront of political activity, they drafted letters to the Dublin Castle administration and petitions to parliament on matters including electoral irregularities, perceived miscarriages of justice, and disputes between locals and officialdom.[37] Father

James Maher attended the Queen's Co. assizes in 1835 to prosecute the conservative voters who had participated in the Graigue election riot, he headed
the call for the investigation into military provocation in Carlow town, and
he was the main instigator of complaints regarding the selection of juries in
the court cases linked to Walsh's murder.[38] John Walsh himself was a political
activist, though despite the London *Times*' description of him as 'a notorious
agitator', he was not one of the clerical political heavyweights. Nonetheless,
he had been deeply involved in political activities, spearheading a parliamentary
petition for the removal of troops from the town of Borris in the immediate
aftermath of the election of June 1835.[39]

Besides being the voice of the local community, priests played a major role
in the preservation of the peace, especially at election time when tempers ran
high and crowds threatened to get out of control. In this respect, James Maher
was probably the single most influential clerical figure among Carlow's
parochial Catholic clergy, followed closely by Martin Doyle of Graigue, both
playing a leading role in preventing mob assaults on conservative supporters
in Carlow town in 1835. The records of the central administration and the
correspondence from its officials at local level support this benign view of the
priests' public role. Sir John Harvey, the Inspector General of Police, fully
acknowledged the positive role of the Carlow priests in preventing violence
at elections and on other occasions, seeing them as the ultimate guardians of
the peace in a volatile society.[40]

Priests were also instrumental in combating agrarian violence at local level,
their considerable influence dissuading displaced tenants and those threatened
by eviction from seeking revenge. Doyle of Graigue had, since the 1820s,
actively worked to prevent agrarian outrage, even to the extent of giving
information against those involved while Maher helped pour oil on troubled
waters after clearances in the Ballinabranna area in 1836.[41] The priest also played
a vital – if unofficial – role in the *cosmhuintir*'s interaction with the law. An
individual wishing to make a sworn statement frequently made his first
approach to the priest, who then accompanied him to the magistrates. In court
the priest sometimes sat near the defendant to give him moral support, as
Father Buggy of Borris did for James Doyle at the perjury trial in the summer
of 1836. Even in less high-profile trials, a character reference from the local
priest could make a great difference to a defendant – even on some occasions
helping to halve the sentence imposed.[42]

A more negative view of the 'political priest', however, was taken by
conservatives. They yearned for the return of the unobtrusive and politically
quiescent priests of the late eighteenth century who 'were not corrupt or
revolutionary … nor did they … debauch the minds of their flocks by filthy
harangues from the Altar or by the publication of indecencies in public
journals'.[43] Some politically active priests they could stomach – even admitting

that Maher of Carlow was 'a useful and zealous clergyman in reforming the morals of the lower classes of society' – but others, like the Fathers Walsh of Borris, were too much to tolerate.[44] Why the Walshs were detested so much more than the truculent Maher is difficult to explain. They had all been involved in the successive campaigns for emancipation, tithe abolition, and electoral and registry control, and had for a decade turned chapels into political arenas, targeting conservative voters (especially those within the Catholic community) through scorching political sermons that stopped just short of incitement to violence. Perhaps it was the family relationship between Walsh and his parish priest uncle that annoyed local conservatives, who referred to the duo derisively as 'the Messrs Walsh'. Or it may have been Walsh's apparent arrogance that provoked them. About a decade younger than Maher or Doyle, Walsh at 35 years of age may have lacked their long experience in striking a balance between the pastoral and the political, and between popular incitement and pacification. Though the duplication of names makes it difficult to distinguish between what uncle and nephew said and did, Walsh junior does seem to have overstepped this boundary on a number of occasions during his ministry in Borris. During the 1832 election he delivered some highly inflammatory sermons against members of his congregation who voted for what he described as the 'grand jury jobber, Bruen' and 'the apostate' Kavanagh, both of whom, despite their clear alignment with the Protestant conservative interest, were good employers and popular landlords – 'good gentlemen to the country at large'.[45] In 1835 Walsh continued to play a major role in fomenting popular resentment (no difficult task) against Catholic conservative voters, his words (allegedly 'that it was no harm to hoot, push or shove' them) leading to a major incident at the end of Sunday mass in early February when a number of these voters were dragged from their pews into the yard and severely beaten by other members of the congregation.[46]

Walsh's zeal seems to have outrun his discretion again a fortnight later with his involvement in memorializing Dublin Castle regarding the stationing of military in Borris during Sunday mass, an issue that, like Walsh's own death a short time later, became the focus for a clash of rival political and denominational loyalties.[47] Walsh argued that the presence of the troops 'at the entrance to the chapel' was a provocation to locals, and he suspended services in the chapel while the troops remained in town.[48] Doyne, the local magistrate responsible for bringing in the troops, argued in turn that the military presence was vital to prevent further attacks on conservative voters in Walsh's own congregation. Moreover, in contradiction to Walsh's claim that the troops were blocking access to the church, he pointed out that it was precisely in order to avoid confrontation that the troops had been stationed indoors, in a public house well out of sight of the church.[49] The Castle investigated the matter carefully, and though it eventually declared in favour of Doyne, it was clear that neither protagonist came credibly out of the dispute and that the rift between the popular and conservative interests in the locality and the county had been further widened. Doyne, though a conscientious magistrate, was no impartial enforcer of the law, being an active conservative and Kavanagh's election agent.[50] Walsh, for his part, seems to have grossly exaggerated both the nearness of the soldiers to the church and their consequent capacity to rouse popular resentment, and despite his claim that the attacks on voters had occurred when he had left the altar and was no longer in control of the crowd, there is little doubt that his own provocative sermons contributed to the violence. Indeed, the confrontational tone of these sermons increased as the June election approached, the most notorious being delivered by him on 17 June and reported (allegedly) verbatim in the *Carlow Sentinel* whose attitude ranged from contempt for 'Fr Jack' to fury against him as a 'seditious ruffian' deserving of the gallows.[51]

It was Walsh's prominent role in the political controversies of the day that led to his being called as a witness before the parliamentary enquiry into the controversial election of June 1835. It was hardly surprising, therefore, that the popular view was that his death, which occurred only a day before he was due to leave for London, was the work of those that wished to prevent him giving evidence against the conservative interest in the county. Though any evidence Walsh could give would surely have reflected as badly on the liberal interests and Catholic clergy as on the Bruen-Kavanagh side, the timing of his death confirmed in the popular mind that the priest had been the murder victim of those who needed to remove from the scene a formidable political opponent.

5. Finding a scapegoat

If Walsh was, in fact, murdered at Kilgraney, why was Archibald Sly targeted as the murderer? The answer lies in a complex mesh of denominational, economic and political issues, land inevitably lying at the core. The election-related issues that caused such conflict among the politicized, had, despite the wild mayhem on polling day, only marginal relevance to the greater part of the rural and urban population. Over 95% of the population had no vote and although they enthusiastically participated in the public drama surrounding elections, their concerns were much more practical, centring largely on access to land and employment. It was these economic issues that were most important in making the Fr Walsh case – or, rather, perceptions of the case – relevant to the smallholders, labourers and miscellaneous poor of the county and beyond.

AGRARIAN ISSUES

Walsh's death occurred at a time when, and in a region where, accelerated changes in landholding were exacerbating rural social tensions. For half a century the population had been rising, and although the statistics before 1851 are extremely unreliable, it appears that between 1821 and 1831 the population of the county increased by just under 4%, and by a further 5% by 1841.[1] Population pressure on land led to the usual desperate struggle for survival in the lower ranks of rural society, the small holders and near landless. The pressure was especially serious in the upland areas along the borders with Wexford to the east, Queen's Co. to the south-west, and in the Rathvilly barony in the north. Here the land was poor and the greater number of holdings averaged 6 acres, and even on farms of up to 20 acres productivity was restricted by the mediocre quality of the soil and by the tendency towards subdivision – a nightmare for landlords trying to collect rents from an increasingly insolvent tenantry.[2] The marginal economy of these uplands stood in contrast to the advanced state of agriculture elsewhere in the county, noted by Lewis as being 'in as highly improved a state … as in any other part of Ireland', the march of improvement ongoing since just after the Napoleonic wars. Yet, even in the better lands, non-payment of rent (for whatever reason) caused major problems, as was the case around Nurney on the Bruen estate where some large farmers defaulted over a long period, leaving the landlord out of pocket by as much as £2,000 by the early 1840s.[3]

It was not surprising, then, that landlords throughout the county tried to counterbalance these problems by promoting more modern farming and rewarding the efforts of progressive producers. Go-ahead landlords like Lord Courtown and Henry Bruen of Oak Park carefully monitored the farming practices of individual tenants.[4] Agricultural societies were established in the county, encouraging the marling of soil, promoting the use of the scotch plough, awarding premiums for the best produce, and holding ploughing competitions that attracted the participation of both large landed proprietors and upwardly mobile farmers.[5] The Borris Farming Society was typical. With the motto 'Speed the plough', it was clearly orientated towards large-scale and modernized farming, and was patronized by the very landlords who were involved in the establishment of large farms locally through clearing swathes of uneconomic small holders, and by the progressive farmers who benefited from those same clearances.

The beneficiaries and practitioners of this new improved farming were of different backgrounds. Some, like Michael Murphy of Sliguff and Ballyellen, were farmers that had built up holdings of up to 200 acres over a few decades.[6] Others were the most able of the previous smallholders, who had been retained on enlarged farms following the displacement of their less competent peers. Still others were brought in from elsewhere in the county or beyond to take the lately cleared land as either freeholders or on lease.[7] There was little doubt that such consolidation resulted in much more efficient and productive farming but it came at a high human cost – that is, the displacement of large numbers of those at the bottom of the rural social pyramid. What the *Carlow Sentinel* described approvingly as the replacement of 'filthy cabins' by 'handsome farm houses' was just the physical manifestation of a major social upheaval.[8] Many dispossessed smallholders were reduced to pauperism or, depending on time and place, to the status of landless labourers working on the land of the larger farmers.[9] On the Courtown Estate in the barony of St Mullins, between Borris and the border of Wexford, such agricultural rationalization led in the mid-1830s to the displacement of 30 families and the consolidation of the vacated lands into five larger holdings.[10] Similar clearances occurred around Rathvilly in the north of the county, while in the latter half of the decade there were further improvement-driven evictions around Ballinabranna, some three miles south-west of Carlow town. Here, according to the admittedly partisan evidence of the local priest, at least 17 families had been cleared, many of them related by blood or marriage – the typical subdividers that were the bane of the improving landlord.[11]

In some places, and to a great extent due to clerical intervention, there was very little protest from the displaced, but in others there resulted a wave of attacks on the property of the larger farmers who had taken the cleared land. The earlier part of the decade had seen major agrarian disturbances as the

Whitefeet reacted to a combination of tithe enforcement, rent increases and land clearances.[12] Attacks of this type – averaging 20 per month in Carlow by the mid-1830s – were motivated by grievances that were purely economic, the displaced making no distinction between consolidating Catholic and Protestant strong farmers, as is clear from the attacks in 1835 on Michael Cullen of Rahana, John Byrne of Harroldstown, and Morgan Dowling of Ballyhackett – all Catholics who had benefited, or were about to benefit, from taking land previously held by smaller farmers.[13] But where sectarian tensions could be tapped, purely economic issues became much more complicated, and this is the context in which the fingering of Archibald Sly for the murder of Fr John Walsh should be viewed.

SECTARIAN ANIMOSITIES

Interdenominational relations in Carlow, as elsewhere, were complex. The denominational composition of the county was akin to that of north Wicklow, Kildare and Queen's Co. (all of which it bordered), with Protestants accounting for approximately 10% of the population, though in some areas amounting to some 40% of the whole.[14] On a day-to-day level, Catholics and Protestants went about their routine business in relative harmony. Protestant farmers employed Catholic labourers and attended the funerals of their workers, Catholic public houses were frequented by Protestants, Catholic and Protestant servants worked together as servants of local gentry, and Protestant and Catholic shopkeepers and millers received custom from both sides of the sectarian divide.[15]

However, sectarian tensions bubbled near the surface, ready to erupt on the slightest pretext. As discussed earlier, constant jockeying for political control meant that there was little love lost between the landed elite on the one hand, and the politically active Catholic clergy and aspiring middle classes on the other. Mutual suspicions were expressed in terms fusing the sectarian and the political, the endangered Protestant elite referring derogatorily to the popular side as the 'popish faction', while the latter responded with references to the 'Orange clan'. This polarization had been growing at an accelerated pace since the 1820s, when the challenge to Protestant hegemony grew with O'Connell's emancipation campaign. It was considerably increased – and spread downwards into the ranks of the *cosmhuintir* – by the popular expectations generated by the Pastorini prophecies, and by resentment (partly spontaneous, partly whipped up by the Catholic clergy) against the evangelism of the 'Second Reformation', so that by the late 1830s a newcomer to Carlow commented in amazement on how 'completely divided' the population was along denominational lines.[16]

But the animosities actually stretched much further back and their expression was shaped by competing historical narratives. The Protestant persecution narratives dating from 1641, emphasizing the inherent disloyalty of Catholics and the fears of the impending 'extermination of Protestantism' were constantly repeated, while the popular side referred back to a past dominated by dispossession and plantation.[17] On both sides, memories of 1798 were still raw. The south of the county had been particularly affected by the rebellion, and the insurgent attacks on Carlow town, on Borris House, the seat of the Kavanaghs, and on the village of Ballickmoyler just across the border in Queen's Co. were still very much within living memory.[18] Both *cosmhuintir* and Protestant media used these events of three decades previously as a lens through which to view more recent occurrences. Street ballads sung around Borris in 1835 recalled

> How our friends did hang and strangle
> [When] in ninety-eight did circulate
> The pitch cap, gibbet and triangles

and, linking the defeat of the past to the expected victory of the future, predicted that 'Bruen and Kavanagh must surrender'.[19] On the other side of the divide, the rhetoric was shaped by the Musgrave-inspired Protestant narrative of the course of the rebellion in Co. Wexford, less than twenty miles to the east. The *Carlow Sentinel* thus described the disturbing sight of the liberal Kildare voters coming into Carlow on polling day in June 1835 as a

> band of rebels ... five abreast in fighting order ... marching through town with as much authority as the rebels of 1798 did after taking Enniscorthy and burning and impaling every Protestant that fell into their hands ... [20]

Such sectarian animosities, permeating every level of society, were exacerbated by the Kilgraney affair. The medical profession, divided between Catholic and liberal on the one hand, and Protestant and conservative on the other, split sharply at the inquest following Walsh's death. Even when it became necessary to draft a map of the area surrounding Kilgreany in preparation for Sly's trial, a draftsman had to be brought in from outside the county to ensure that justice was seen to be done, since 'it would be impossible to get a person devoid of party feelings in this part of the country'.[21] In the police force, too, divisions that had existed for some time were also deepened by the affair. Tension increased between the old Peace Preservation Force – its numbers declining drastically in the early 1830s – and the newer County Constabulary, sardonically – and inaccurately – dubbed 'O'Connell's police' by Protestant conservatives.[22] Even in the latter force, tensions increased between Catholic constables and Protestant sergeants, and between Protestant and Catholic members of the rank-and-file, so much so that when Sly's trial came up in March 1836, the stipendary magistrate considered it necessary to draft in police from another county 'to do the duty at the assizes, as the local police being so long resident in the county must more or less be imbued with the violent party feeling which pervades all classes in that unhappy county'.[23]

Even the army was infected by sectarian division. This was what lay behind the public disturbances that erupted in Carlow town in August 1835 when soldiers of the 1st Royal Dragoons and the 91st Foot became involved in confrontations with the crowd. Allegations and counter-allegations flew forward and back regarding the use of party slogans by the soldiers – 'Priests' skins on Orangemen's houses' – and the populace – 'Give us the head of an Orangeman!' Even more significantly, in view of recent events, one witness swore that soldiers involved in hauling bundles of hay in the barracks were working to the rhythm of 'Pull, pull, as the devil is pulling Priest Walsh's head into hell'.[24] The animosities that inspired such exchanges between soldiery and populace soaked right up through the social hierarchy. In the investigation that followed the army-crowd confrontations, Catholic witnesses took the popular side, while the military were supported by all the established Protestant magistrates. The division was not entirely clear-cut, since three Catholic men of substance, along with the very balanced stipendary magistrate, Walter Moloney, denied that the soldiers' behaviour had been provocative.[25] But the further down the social scale one went, the more bitter the animosity. If the towns were no havens of toleration, the rural areas could prove just as prone to disturbance when sectarian meshed with agrarian resentments. It was precisely such a fusion of the agrarian and the sectarian that brought Archibald Sly into the Walsh drama.

The social tensions created by the improvement-orientated clearances in the county in the 1830s were obviously exacerbated in those cases where the displaced smallholders were Catholic, and where the farmer beneficiaries were Protestant. On the Courtown estate the 30 families being targeted for clearance in the mid-1830s (and finally cleared in 1839) were all Catholic, while four of the five strong farmers put in their place were Protestants from Queen's Co.[26] More immediately relevant to the Walsh case was the bitterness caused in 1831 by removal of 15 Catholic smallholders from the so-called 'Beresford's triangle' centred on the townland of Sliguff beside Kilgraney bridge, and their replacement by a number of Protestant families including the Wynnes, Styles and Slys.[27] How sweeping the clearance was is not entirely clear, though Griffith's Valuation, completed in Carlow in 1853, shows a preponderance of 'Protestant' surnames among the townland's 21 occupiers a decade after the changes had been made.[28] Unlike the case on the Courtown estate, it is not at all clear to what extent these Protestant tenants had come 'from outside'. They may well have been new to Sliguff, but their roots seem to have been within the county, and at no great distance from their new holdings. Archibald Sly, eventually tried for Walsh's murder, had got land in Sliguff but his home farm was no further away than Carrignafecca, some five miles to the north-west, where he had resided since at least the mid-1820s.[29]

Though such replacements were largely due to a belief in the more progressive attitude of Protestant farmers, there was also a political motivation. This was the conviction that the settlement at local level of Protestant farmers, dependable conservative voters, was the best guarantee of security when, as the *Carlow Sentinel* put it, 'the interests of the community are at stake and the institutions of the empire on the eve of overthrow by those demagogues whom the priests return to parliament'.[30] The economic and the political motivations for land clearance and resettlement were thus closely intermeshed. This would appear to have been the case at Sliguff. There the clearances were obviously improvement-driven since most of the farms were very extensive – from 50 to almost 120 acres – and the fields were large and regularly shaped. But the clearances had also served Lord Beresford's purpose to punish the former tenants who had, under the influence of the priests, opposed Kavanagh and Bruen in the election of 1832.[31] Threats of similar election-related clearance were made by John Alexander around Tullowcreen between Leighlinbridge and the Queen's Co. border, and it also seems to have been to the forefront of Henry Bruen's mind in the late 1830s when he and his agent carefully noted in his estate papers the 'rent due by tenants who voted for O'Connell' and prepared a list of which freeholders should be pressed for that rent or served with a notice to quit.[32] Similarly, on the Ballinabranna estate, in the bailiwick of Fr James Maher, clearance that had already begun as part of a consolidation process was now directed at 22 tenants who had voted for the popular candidates in June 1835.[33]

But in land-related disputes, it was never clear whether the political took precedence over the economic, or *vice versa*. The authorities were not far off the mark when they concluded that some of the faceless attacks on freeholders to punish them for – or deter them from – voting conservative were really motivated by grievances about the taking of land from which others had been removed.[34] Similarly, when freeholders who had voted O'Connellite were pressed for rent arrears or threatened with eviction, the landlord may have been more concerned with availing of a God-given chance to recoup financial losses or get rid of troublesome tenants than with teaching 'the serfs' a political lesson.[35] Bruen, in the aftermath of the June election of 1835 made careful note not only of those who had 'voted with the priest' but also those 'displaying a want of system and regularity [and] … who [though] undoubtedly able to pay leave some more some less of their half year's rent unpaid'.[36]

Whatever the motive, clearances from which Protestant tenants benefited at the expense of Catholics were bound to rouse popular begrudgery on a grand scale.[37] Archibald Sly and a number of his fellow Protestant farmers were certainly targets of such begrudgery. They had at least two farms each in the neighbourhood of Sliguff and Kilgraney, freeholds with valuations ranging between £10 and £50. The scale of their agricultural activities seems to have gone well beyond the hand-to-mouth existence of the small farmer, since they employed labourers and either bred sheep or grew corn on such a scale as to require a sizeable number of reapers.[38] They occupied, in effect, the lower levels of the Protestant elite, certainly not ascendancy themselves, but sharing in the political and religious values of that class. All of them had gun licences – nothing exceptional, it must be stressed, since Catholic farmers, priests and gentlemen also appeared on the licence holder lists – but the *attitude* to this right to bear arms does appear to have set them apart from many others equally entitled to do so, and surely attracted the animosity of other locals.[39] Gentlemen, that is, those generally listed as 'esquire' in the newspaper reports and trade directories of the day, had long presumed the entitlement to carry weapons in public places – something evident during the election of June 1835 when the magistrates found it necessary to advise a number of Protestant gentlemen to take a more discreet approach to self-protection.[40] But this cavalier attitude to carrying arms was evident much further down the social hierarchy of Carlow Protestants. This became apparent in 1836 when a Protestant named Kelly appeared before the magistrates, charged with carrying an unlicensed carbine at Altana on the previous 12 July. The differences arising between the magistrates on the matter was very much a clash between the old world and the new – Protestant ascendancy and the 'impartial state'. Hamilton and Staples, the local Justices of the Peace, claimed that Kelly's Protestantism was his automatic entitlement to bear arms, since

> the 19th Geo 2nd chap 14 – authorizes and empowers all persons of the Protestant Religion to carry arms, and that therefore this Kelly being of that persuasion could not be fined under the Act for preventing improper persons from carrying arms.[41]

The third magistrate, Walter Moloney, a stipendary appointee of the central administration, hastily corresponded with Dublin Castle, the reply confirming (as he had expected) that the law relating to arms licensing applied 'to all persons without reference to their religion'. But the fact that the issue had been brought up in the first place showed just how slowly old habits and attitudes died out at local level where legal and social changes were fought tooth and nail by an endangered denominational elite, both exalted and plebeian.

ORANGEMEN AND YEOMEN

The fact that the contested question of bearing and using arms on this occasion
was linked to the celebrations of 12 July underlines the importance locally of
another major controversy affecting Carlow, as the rest of the island, in the
mid-1830s, that is, the future of the Orange Order. An object of the
unwelcome attention of the reforming Whig administration, the Order's
increasing vulnerability was brought home strongly to Carlow Protestants by
the dismissal in late 1835 of a number of Protestant policemen in New Ross
because of their alleged membership of an Orange lodge. As New Ross was
just 15 miles distant over the Wexford border, the incident roused a mixture
of popular triumphalism and intense Protestant resentment in Carlow,
colouring the attitude of, and the local reaction to, Protestant farmers like
Archibald Sly.[42] It was, therefore, to be expected that in the contemporary
popular narrative of Walsh's death, there was considerable stress on the Orange
links of the alleged killers. The ballads referred to 'the Orange clan' and the
sermon delivered after the Kilgraney affair by Walsh's uncle, the parish priest
of Borris, openly stated that the younger man had been murdered by
Orangemen.

This emphasis on the Orangeman as the enemy was derived partly from
local memories of 1798 when the members of some six Orange lodges in the
county had been actively involved in combating the rebellion and – more
importantly – when the terms 'orange' and 'protestant' came to be used
interchangeably as hate labels among the *cosmhuintir*.[43] But more recent events
also played their part in rousing mutual hatreds and rending the thin veil of
everyday toleration. The self-dissolution of the Orange Order in February
1836, in response to the concerted opposition of the Whig government, struck
Orangemen throughout the island – especially those below the ranks of the
gentry – with considerable dismay. Feeling betrayed by the government, and
humiliated by the delighted crowing of their local opponents, they reacted
with defiant and provocative demonstrations. In the Carlow context, these
tensions were aggravated by the death of Walsh and, more specifically, by the
controversy surrounding the arrest and trial of Archibald Sly. As always, local
animosities were increased by news of events elsewhere, and especially by
occurrences just across the county bounds in Wexford and Queen's Co. where
the celebration of 12 July – and the popular reaction to it – threatened to
cause major disruption, particularly in 1836. The atmosphere was especially
tense in Durrow where 'a rather extensive' lodge existed and where military
patrols were considered necessary to keep the peace on the night of the
celebrations. The same preventive measures were needed in Portarlington
where 'a very bad spirit' prevailed between opposing mobs when an Orange
bonfire at Deer Park was prevented by military patrols.[44] Even more volatile

was the atmosphere in the vicinity of Newtownbarry just over the Wexford border. This area was already a natural flashpoint for sectarian hatreds due to the much-sung-about tithe incident there half a decade previously, but the combined issues of Walsh's death and the dissolution of the Orange Order made matters even more explosive, with the celebration of both the Twelfth and Guy Fawkes seeing the defiant flying of flags from the Protestant church, the ornamentation of its walls with boughs and orange lilies, and the firing of shots from the nearby Lord Farnham's demesne.[45]

Moreover, some of the Orange lodges in these counties seem to have stuck their oar particularly deeply into the political affairs of Carlow – hardly surprising, considering the very short distance between the places involved. One lodge from Queen's Co. appears to have taken an active part in the controversial Carlow election of June 1835, a group of its members (some of them holding a vote in Carlow) taking part in a provocative procession that ended up in the riot at Graigue, just outside Carlow town, the details of which were, as usual, clouded by contradictory evidence.[46] Spokesmen for the Queen's Co. men claimed that there was nothing to distinguish them as Orangemen, though they did not actually deny that they belonged to an Orange lodge, and were actually headed by a leading member of the Queen's Co. Grand Lodge. They also argued, probably not inaccurately, that the trouble originated in an attack by a huge crowd composed of 'individuals of the lowest class belonging to the town of Graigue' who had jeered them and pelted them with stones and roof slates. In the counter-claims by the Graigue crowd and its supporters, the stones became 'pebbles' and the fracas originated in the provocation offered by the incoming group who had reputedly marched four deep over the bridge shouting 'No Surrender!' The debate continued from the Carlow petty sessions, where the Graigue side prosecuted the Orange interlopers, to the petty sessions in Ballickmoyler just over the Queen's Co. border, where roles were reversed and the Queen's Co. men took on the role of prosecutors.[47]

In most respects, the Graigue clash was simply one of the many 'storm-in-a-teacup' party confrontations that caused major headaches to local magistrates and police, and led Castle officials to shake their heads wearily at the difficulties of bringing reform to the provinces. But even the totally contradictory evidence involved actually casts considerable light on local party alignments and enhances our understanding of the context of, and fallout from, the death of John Walsh a few weeks later. Firstly, though the social composition of the group coming in from Queen's Co. was never clearly described, it is almost certain that it represented more than one level of Protestant society – whose common bond, if not membership of an Orange lodge, was a shared fear of the consequences of political reform. One can see this in the mode of transport used in that journey in from Queen's Co. to Carlow. The gentry figures like

Barker Thacker of Ballymeelish and William Buller Scott of Anne Grove, all themselves Justices of the Peace, drove to Carlow in their own carriages, while other slightly more humble freeholders travelled together in the brake lent by Lord de Vesci. But there was also the rank-and-file who, if we believe the popular report, 'marched' in, shouted offensive slogans, and were not at all averse when under fire from the Graigue crowd, of replying with their own shower of stones. The same social gradation is revealed in the different ways they formally registered their complaints against the Graigue attackers. While the gentlemen with country seats wrote indignant but measured letters to Dublin Castle to state their case, the humbler individuals headed for the petty sessions – the usual source of legal redress for the non-elite.[48] That they chose the petty sessions of Ballickmoyler as the arena in which to prosecute the Graigue crowd was partly a practical matter – it was the normal sessions for their area. But it was also because the Queen's Co. magistrates were known to have stronger Orange sympathies than those of Carlow, something reflected not only in the number of magistrates who had been in the group at Graigue, but also in the decision of the Carlow magistrates (no friends to liberalism themselves) to transfer the case to a higher court rather than trying it at the petty sessions.[49]

But how active was Orangeism in Carlow itself? By the mid-1830s there was no obvious sign of the six lodges that had existed in the county in 1798. In fact, a house of commons report noted that the there was no Grand Lodge for the county, and that local Orangemen were actually linked to three lodges outside the county – one in Wicklow and two in Wexford.[50] Yet the popular view was that both the influence and the extent of Orangeism in the region were considerable. A complaint in 1836 to the Castle from the village of Kiledmond in the south east of the county spoke of the occurrence 'for some time back' of nightly Orange meetings accompanied by the making of offensive speeches, the singing of provocative songs and the firing of shots. Although no further evidence of Orange organization in the county appeared, the establishment of a new Wexford Orange lodge at Newtownbarry in May 1835, less than a year before the Order dissolved, supports the official view that Carlow Protestants were joining lodges in neighbouring counties.[51]

Whether Archibald Sly and the others accused of Fr Walsh's murder were actually Orangemen or not is unclear. They certainly were politically conservative Protestants, all supporting the candidacy of Bruen and Kavanagh in the recent elections, and forming a small, tight-knit community in which blood, marriage or acquaintance linked farmers with the household staff and estate management of ascendancy and gentry households. Sly's nephew, for instance, worked as a servant in Borris House, and accompanied the Kavanagh family on their holiday in Italy in early 1836. Sly himself, along with his brother, seems to have been actively involved with Kavanagh's estate manager in the breaking of leases as part of the campaign to wipe out the O'Connellite vote after the June election of 1835.[52] But were they members of the Orange Order? Probably yes, but there is currently no evidence to confirm this. The most his enemies could say about Sly was that he was 'a reputed Orangeman', and the constant use of terms like 'Orange faction' and 'Orangemen' in relation to local Protestants may simply indicate that the word 'Orange' was just the common shorthand for 'ultra-Protestant' and thus tell us as much about popular fears and prejudices as it does about the political affiliations of Archibald Sly and his peers.

Putative Orange links aside, there was another reason for Sly et al. to figure high on the popular hate list. They were also apparently members of the yeomanry, of whom there were 438 in the county in 1834 – a number equivalent to that in the average Ulster county, and larger than that in many larger counties in Munster and Leinster. The largest company in Carlow was that at Cloydah and Killeshin, just across the county boundary from the Queen's Co. 'Orange' village of Ballickmoyler.[53] In the popular imagination the yeomanry were associated with the suppression of the 1798 rebellion, largely because they had been a predominantly Protestant force at the time and because their membership had overlapped with that of the Orange lodges.[54] By the 1830s the force, which had been re-activated to deal with anti-tithe disturbances, was still closely associated with ultra-Protestantism, and in south-east Leinster had earned itself a particularly bad press through the trigger-happy behaviour of the troop at Newtownbarry who, breaking under a shower of stones from anti-tithe rioters in June 1831, opened fire and killed 12 protestors.[55] Though the yeomanry was almost defunct again by the time of Walsh's death, former members were not allowed to forget that they were enemies of 'the people'. The Sliguff Protestants, who had almost certainly been yeomen, were described in 1836 as 'heroes of Newtownbarry notoriety', but as was frequently the case with such blanket accusations, this was a distortion of reality. The government enquiry showed that while a troop of yeomanry and a magistrate from the east Carlow village of Myshall had indeed been present at Newtownbarry, none of those from the Sliguff area had any recorded part in the incident.[56] Facts, however, were not allowed to get in the way of popular anti-Protestant feeling, and the animosity was increased by the fact that members of the now disbanded yeomanry in Carlow continued to hold their muskets. This gave the Protestant side the advantage in local party clashes, as happened in Carlow town in late September 1835 when tempers were running high about the Walsh affair. A violent mob attack on Wright's public house, a watering hole for local Orangemen, almost turned into another Newtownbarry when a group of local yeomen arrived to restore order and they and the publican's son fired into the street. No casualties occurred, but both the incident itself and the ensuing court case showed the level and volatility of party feeling in the town: four rioters were convicted, and the bench's condoning of the use of firearms by the defenders only served to fan the flames of party bitterness.[57]

But if the party affiliations and land acquisition of the Sliguff Protestant farmers made them the focus of popular suspicions following Walsh's death, why was Sly particularly singled out from among his alleged accomplices as the one most implicated in the alleged murder? All were tarred equally as Orangemen and yeomen, yet it was Sly that was fingered as having struck the fatal blow at Kilgraney. Perhaps he was, in fact, the killer. But if the entire story was a fiction he may have been singled out simply because his personality invited or even courted popular hatred. He was the individual – something like John Walsh on the other side of the political divide – that his opponents loved to hate. The liberal press implied that Sly was arrogant and provocative in his behaviour and, despite the undoubtedly partisan character of the source, the claim may not have been entirely unfounded. He seems to have been at loggerheads with others in the neighbourhood for well over a decade. In 1824 he was attacked by a group of locals at Knocklonigad near Carrignafecka, the reason for the attack being unclear but the spearheading of the attack by five individuals of the same surname (Curren) suggesting that land occupancy was involved.[58] In 1837, a year after his acquittal for Walsh's murder, there was another incident in which his apparently belligerent attitude led to a court case between himself and three other locals when, on his way home from Tullow, he had a major altercation with three men who were walking along singing (presumably party) songs. The details of the clash were, as usual, extremely unclear, but Sly, who seems to have drawn his pistol and ridden his horse at the three, then brought them before the next assizes on an unsuccessful and apparently grossly inflated charge of 'conspiracy to murder'.[59] Described by the extremely unfriendly Morning Chronicle – with what authority is not at all clear – as a 'person of very violent character', Archibald Sly seems to have had the unfortunate knack of making a bad situation even worse.[60] It seems reasonable to suggest that it was this personality trait that made him a likely target for popular hostility, even if he never laid a finger on Fr John Walsh. Then there was his involvement in the campaign to unseat the victorious popular candidates after the June election of 1835. He was actively involved, along with Kavanagh's steward, Cardiff, in identifying voters on the O'Connellite side whose valuations had been (reputedly) inflated, and in identifying loopholes in registrations – something guaranteed to draw popular animosity.[61] There is also evidence that Sly's natural truculence was increased by alcohol. At his trial in 1836 it was stated by his own nephew that Sly was 'in liquor' when he left Borris shortly before the death of Walsh and when he clashed with the three men on the road from Tullow in 1837 both he and they had been drinking – something which undoubtedly contributed to the ill feeling between them. Indeed, despite his claim in court on that occasion that he 'never was drunk in his life ... but he might have been tipsy', one is left with the sense that in Sly's case alcohol and natural testiness were a dangerous combination.[62]

6. Into the future

In one way, Fr John Walsh's death in 1835 was something of a nine-days' wonder. Despite hitting the headlines locally, nationally and throughout the British Isles, the controversy died down relatively quickly. The reports to the Castle on ballads about the event tailed off within a very short time of the death, and once Sly had been acquitted and the perjury trials completed, the matter faded from the newspapers.

LOCALITY AND WIDER WORLD

But for the individuals involved, the matter was far from over. The main witnesses against Sly fared badly. The youngest of them, Patrick Fleming, apparently escaped transportation because he confessed (at what stage is not entirely clear) that he had perjured himself in court, but Rooney, Doyle and Corrigan were transported and there is at present no trace of their subsequent lives in Australia.[1] Nor does Archibald Sly seem to have fared very well in the aftermath of the controversy. Popular animosity against him continued: threats were made against anyone who worked for him, and in one particularly dramatic incident in 1838 the funeral of one of his workmen at Clonegal cemetery was seriously disrupted when the body was reputedly disinterred by a hostile crowd and thrown on the roadside.[2] Financially, too, Sly seems to have been in bad straits following his four months' imprisonment when he was unable to oversee his farm, so much so that seven months after his acquittal it was considered necessary to call for subscriptions for his relief through the columns of the *Carlow Sentinel*.[3] While this subscription appeal appears to have been as much a way of whipping up animosity against the popular side as of baling Sly out financially, it does appear in hindsight that he did, indeed, have major problems: two decades after Walsh's death, when Griffith's Valuation was completed for Carlow, Sly had disappeared from the townland of Sliguff and now held land – a mere 17 acres – at Milltown in the neighbouring civil parish of Fennagh.[4] Sixty years later, again, when the census of 1911 was complied, although the names of others accused of complicity in the priest's death were still to be found in the locality, the Sly surname had completely disappeared.[5]

Outside the personal experience of those involved, the Kilgraney incident continued to cast its shadow. Two competing narratives emerged, one centring on 'the murdered Father Walsh', the other on the 'heart-rending case of

Archibald Sly'.[6] At popular level, nothing could shake the conviction that a murder had occurred. Over a year after Walsh's death, Catholic priests in Carlow were warned against travelling alone through Sliguff lest they share his fate, and when O'Connell visited Carlow during the election of 1841, he took care to include in his speech a reference to Walsh's 'murder'.[7] On the Protestant side, an equally firm conviction persisted that the fingering of Sly was part of an ongoing persecution of Irish Protestants, at the heart of which was a priestly conspiracy, even the judge at the trials of both Sly and Anne Rooney intimating – 'there is yet a mystery upon the whole proceeding' – that sinister hidden forces were at work.[8] The incident reflected the expectations and fears aroused in an age of dramatic political, religious and social change. Within the county of Carlow and in the broader Irish context, it raised questions not only about jury composition, the administration of justice and popular attitudes to perjury, but also about sectarian tensions, agrarian problems, social order and the nature of political representation. Most importantly, it was part of the accelerating leadership struggle between traditional and aspiring elites – landed proprietors (largely but not totally Protestant) on the one hand, and the Catholic middle classes and clergy on the other. The struggle did not end with the Walsh affair. The later years of the 1830s were even more disturbed, with major tensions between central administration and local elites concerning control of the police, the appointment and dismissal of magistrates, the drafting of jury lists and the registration of voters – all issues that had, in one way or another, been intermeshed with the incident at Kilgraney.[9]

Outside the immediate region, the death of a provincial Catholic curate and the trial of a local Protestant farmer – no matter how prominent in the small pond of Carlow affairs – might not have been expected to attract much attention. But interest was aroused far beyond the immediate local context because the Kilgraney incident became an act in the larger drama in which rival forces clashed – traditionalism and ultra-Protestantism on the one hand, and the liberal reforming state on the other. The newspaper reporting of the unfolding saga, therefore, was not really about provincial politics in Carlow but concerned much more fundamental and ongoing debates about power in the United Kingdom and beyond. Liberal journals like the *Morning Chronicle* emphasized Sly's belligerence to show that ultra-Protestantism in the Irish and broader context was self-serving and destructive. On the other hand, staunchly conservative papers like the *Times* of London and the *Belfast Newsletter* focussed on what they saw as the state's mishandling of Sly's case. Stressing especially the refusal to grant bail and the countenancing of apparently perjured information, they emphasized how supine the Whig government was in the face of priestly and liberal pressure – an argument taken up by Lord Brougham in the house of lords in 1839. Ultra-Protestant prints like *Blackwood's* and

Fraser's magazines centred, as did their political equivalents nearer home, on the 'popish plot' interpretation of the story and warned that Irish 'papists' were at heart traitors, persecutors and perjurers, not to be trusted with any increased political power.[10]

WHAT HAPPENED?

But what really happened at Kilgraney bridge? Irrespective of the different 'definitive' conclusions reached by the inquest and the successive trials, there is no way of knowing. Only two certainties emerge out of the puzzle. The first is that Fr John Walsh of Borris died at Kilgraney sometime before 11 o'clock on that July night in 1835. The second is that historical sources mask as much as they reveal. The least dramatic and most probable explanation is that Walsh died as a result of being thrown by his reputedly skittish horse when his short-sightedness caused him to miss the sharp turn on the road. It is feasible that when he was thrown, his head hit the bridge parapet with force, resulting in the deep head wound that caused his death. But the inquest verdict dismissed the possibility of an accident. Not only did the medical men initially decide that Walsh's injuries were deliberately inflicted, but nobody at that inquest had noticed any sharp or protruding stones in the bridge structure that could cause the two-by-three inch wound on Walsh's head. Nor does this theory tally with the evidence that the blood spatters on the bridge wall looked as if they had fallen from a height. But, as contemporary Protestant objections showed, the jurors at the inquest may have lacked the objectivity needed to seriously consider the possibility of an accident, while the witnesses – from priests to landless labourers – were sufficiently shocked and excited by the death to envisage a worst-case scenario.

Perhaps Walsh's death did indeed result from his head striking the bridge wall, but perhaps this was not entirely the result of an accident. Maybe the horse shied and threw Walsh when frightened by a group lying in wait in the shadows – the group seen at the bridge earlier in the night by one of the most credible witnesses at the inquest, whose evidence was given relatively little attention. Had that group (if it ever existed) planned, possibly under the effects of alcohol, to teach Walsh a lesson for his political interference and to caution him as to his statements at the upcoming election enquiry? Was the lesson to take the form of a little rough handling – nothing new in the repertoire of agrarian and sectarian 'heavies' at the time – and was Walsh's death from a head injury simply a by-product of their ambush misfiring?

Or did the group actually set upon Walsh and, as the evidence of the alleged perjurers described it, pull him from his horse – though not before the frantic priest had given Sly a blow of his whip on the nose – and allow Styles to 'finish him off' with a hammer? Did they kick him when he was on the ground as that evidence also alleged? If so, how was the body (as the inquest doctors had described) free of any marks except for the head wound and the bruise on the left palm? If Walsh was 'finished off' on the ground, where did that leave the story of the blood apparently coming from a height? But if the blood did come from above, it is difficult to envisage how an attacker on foot could inflict a heavy blow on the head of a man on horseback. What height was the horse? No questions were asked about this, or if they were, they remained unrecorded.

If one of the men did batter Walsh, which one did it? The evidence of Doyle, Corrigan and Fleming put Styles in the role of hammer man, but also quoted Sly as claiming that he had done the deed, while the story told by Rooney (admittedly by far the least dependable of a very undependable foursome) gave all three men a direct role in the killing, adding a second instrument (a crowbar) for good measure. How were the instruments of death disposed of? Doyle implied in court that Sly had said in his earshot that he had got rid of the hammer, but there was (hardly surprisingly) no mention of a crowbar.

Or, to return once again to the theory of an accidental death, were all these stories false, and was Sly the unsuspecting victim of a conspiracy? This, too, is very likely, since his religion, his acquisition of land, his political involvement and his personality made him a likely target for popular animosity. If he was targeted thus, was this the result of some 'popish plot', as some newspapers described it? Certainly, the conservative interest generally, in Carlow and beyond, was in no doubt that behind this alleged plot were the politically active priests of the county – among whom Walsh himself had been numbered. Young Patrick Fleming's admission that he had perjured himself could be taken as proof that there had been some directing hand behind the 'creation' of the evidence. But did he confess simply to avoid transportation? He seems not to have identified any individual string puller and, in view of the prevalence of conspiracy theories among ultra-Protestants in pre-Famine Ireland, one is tempted to dismiss this version of events as a symptom of political and sectarian paranoia. But the incongruity of the evidence against Sly makes one rethink. While containing a number of internal contradictions, the three stories from Corrigan, Doyle and Fleming dovetailed closely. The stories may, therefore, have been true. But if they were fabricated – either in whole or in part – then the consistencies between them strongly suggest some guiding hand behind the scene. Was there a priestly conspiracy to get at Sly through perjured evidence – not at all inconceivable in a period of intense political and social unrest? Indeed, there are hints that Fr James Maher, in particular, had no trouble in massaging the truth when the occasion demanded.[11] Or were there some widely known but unproven reports locally about what 'actually happened' at Kilgraney, reports that needed fashioning into a more coherent narrative if, even at the risk of perjury, the killers of Walsh were to be convicted? On the other hand, if the stories were true, then was there an equivalent conspiracy on the Protestant side – a conspiracy to ensure, come what may, that the law did not fall heavily on 'one of the right sort'.[12]

If Walsh was murdered at Kilgraney, there is no doubt that the motive was both political and sectarian since, though not one of the most prominent 'political priests' of his day, he had made himself obnoxious to the beleaguered conservative interest in the county by his prominent and provocative role in emergent O'Connellite politics. If, on the other hand, Walsh's death was accidental, then the framing of Archibald Sly as his murderer was the outcome of an even more complex motivational mix – begrudgery against a successful farmer, sectarian bitterness against a member of a slipping but still cocky Protestant plebeian elite, and – it also appears – intense personal dislike of a character who, like the man he purportedly killed, was prone to excess in the cause he followed. Either way, what the tragedy showed – and there were no winners – was that in times of political and social crisis when internal divisions were bridged by fear of a common enemy, rival communities closed ranks and looked after their own.

Conclusion: Remembering

For some time after Walsh's death, the memory was kept alive by the building of a small cairn constantly replenished by pebbles placed upon it by passers-by, but the story seems to have receded into oblivion thereafter.[1] Perhaps this was predictable considering that the incident was the product of particular circumstances at a particular time, no longer relevant when those times and circumstances had passed. Whether the ravages of the famine on the *cosmhuintir* of Carlow and south Leinster played a part in erasing the memory is not clear, for while the Irish Folklore Commission collectors in the 1930s gathered a number of memories on the 1798 rebellion in the county, the Fr Walsh story does not appear to have figured in the material collected. Yet, it was precisely during the Commission's lifetime, when the centenary of the priest's death approached, that the story surfaced again with the unveiling of the monument at Kilgraney bridge in August 1836. Over the course of a century very little had changed. The approach to Kilgraney bridge was identical to that mapped in the aftermath of Fr Walsh's death in 1835. The road was as narrow as ever, the right-angled bend was still there, and the wall of the bridge was still intact. Besides, the landscape of memory had apparently remained as unchanged as the physical one, since the monument was placed (with due regard for increasing traffic) on almost the exact spot where John Walsh's body had been found in the early morning of 31 July one hundred years before. Unfortunately, in the current state of research, it is not clear where those organizing the monument project got their information on the events they commemorated – perhaps from local memory, perhaps from old newspapers. The inscription on the monument was simple and factual:

> Pray for the repose of the soul of Rev. John Walsh, C.C., Borris (1823–1835) whose dead body was found at this place 31st July 1835, and who, according to the verdict of a Coroner's Jury, was killed by a person or persons unknown.

At the laying of the foundation stone a year previously, there had been some pointed phrases regarding 'martyrdom', 'foul murder' and 'alien ascendancy'. But the speeches in 1936 were, though decidedly Catholic in their devotional references, measured and politically non-divisive. However, there was a subtext. The inscription, by recording the inquest's judgment had implicitly taken sides and had gone much further in identifying its sympathies than had the original

discreet memorial tablet in Borris Catholic church, erected at some undefined
date in the 19th century, and simply noted that Walsh 'departed this life the
30th of July 1835'.[2] Thus, the centenary organizers had, in harmony with the
accepted image of Ireland in the 1930s, done what most commemorations do.
They had transformed the context of Walsh's death from the intricate mix of
political competition, sectarian animosity and agrarian tension of the 1830s to
one of a clear-cut confrontation between persecution and patriotism and had,
unconsciously following the pattern of the event they commemorated,
transformed the unproven into fact.

Notes

ABBREVIATIONS

CSORPPI   Chief Secretary's Office, Registered Papers, Private Index (National Archives of Ireland)

CSORPOR   Chief Secretary's Office, Registered Papers, Outrage Reports (National Archives of Ireland)

CS   *Carlow Sentinel*

FJ   *Freeman's Journal*

NLI   National Library of Ireland, Dublin

SOC   State of the Country Papers (National Archives of Ireland)

1. A BODY AT KILGRANEY

1 *Nationalist* (Carlow), 27 July, 1 Aug. 1935, 3 Aug. 1936.

2 *FJ*, 10 Aug. 1835.

3 *Times*, 10 Aug. 1835; *CS*, 10 Mar. 1836.

4 *CS*, 1 Aug. 1835; *FJ*, 23 Aug. 1839. I have used the modern spelling of Sliguff, though in most of the sources for the 1830s the townland was spelt as Slyguff.

5 *FJ*, 18 Mar. 1835, 27 Nov. 1835; CSORPPI, Carlow, 1835, 25/1053: Walter Moloney, Resident Magistrate, to Morpeth, 18 Nov. 1835; 203/1/1, Walter Moloney to Drummond, 25 Feb. 1836.

6 CSORPPI, Carlow, 1836, 3/400, Vignoles to Drummond, 17 Mar. 1836.

7 A detailed examination of the political involvement of John Murphy and his priest-uncle, another John, was completed by the late Tom Murphy of Borris. The present work is very much indebted to Murphy's exhaustive collection of source material from contemporary newspapers and other sources. Tom Murphy, *The Fathers Walsh of Borris: political intrigue, murder and transportation in the 1830s* (Kilkenny, 2007); *Nationalist* (Carlow), 20 February 2008.

8 Murphy, *The Fathers Walsh*, p. 5.

9 S.J. Connolly, *Priests and people in pre-Famine Ireland* (Dublin, 1982), pp 65–71.

10 *CS*, 19 Mar. 1836.

11 *FJ*, 31 July 1835; *CS*, 23 Mar. 1836.

12 *FJ*, 19 Mar. 1836; *Fraser's Magazine for Town and Country*, 13 (Jan.-June 1836), p. 513.

13 *An alphabetical list of persons who have registered votes pursuant to the Act of the 2nd and 3rd of William IV, chap. 88, to the 1st day of February, 1838*. Carlow County – Ireland Genealogical Projects (IGP), http://www.Irish Genealogical Projects (accessed 4 Dec. 2009). *Griffith's Valuation*, Province of Leinster, Co. Carlow, parish of Lorum, p. 230. Although Sly no longer occupied the farm at Carrignafecka when the primary valuation was completed, the single farm there (98 acres in extent) was held in fee by Henry Newton who apparently was Sly's landlord in 1835.

14 CSORPPI, Carlow 1835, 4/1053, Moloney to Dublin Castle, 11 Aug. 1835.

2. THE CASTLE AND THE WALSH CASE

1 CSORPPI, Carlow 1835, 2/203, Joseph Greene, Kilkenny to Dublin Castle, 28 June 1835.

2   CSORPPI, Carlow, 1835, 3/1053,
    Moloney to Castle, 3 Aug. 1835; *CS*, 8
    Aug. 1835; *FJ*, 21 Mar. 1836.
3   *FJ*, 5 Aug. 1835.
4   *FJ*, 21 Mar. 1836; CSORPPI, Carlow,
    1835, 3/1053, Moloney RM to Castle,
    3 Aug. 1835; 1836, 14/1053, 9 Mar.
    1836. McCredy and Bate, attorneys, to
    Dublin Castle, seeking attendance of
    Dr Rawson of the County Carlow
    Infirmary and Surgeon Miller of the
    57th Regiment at Sly's trial.
5   CSORPPI, Carlow, 1835, 1053/19.
    Walter Newton, Bagtenalstown, to
    Drummond, 7 Aug. 1835.
6   *Times* (London), 10 Aug. 1835.
7   CSORPPI, Carlow 1835, 6/1053,
    James Battersby, Sub-Inspector,
    Carlow, to Dublin Castle, 16 Aug.
    1835.
8   CSORPPI, Carlow 1835, 1053/23,
    Chief Constable Hawkshaw to Sub
    Inspector, 6 Oct. 1835; CSORPOR,
    Carlow, 1835, 31/3, 23 Aug. 1835, 'To
    the Patriots of Leighlin Bridge'; *CS*, 29
    Aug. 1835.
9   CSORPPI, Carlow 1835, 1053/3,
    Moloney to Dublin Castle, 3 Aug.
    1835; 1053/5, Moloney to Castle, 14
    Aug. 1835; 1053/11, Hugh Murray,
    Sub Constable, to Sub-Inspector, 31
    July 1835; 1063/6, James Battersby to
    Dublin Castle, 15 Aug. 1835; *CS*, 10
    Feb. 1836; *FJ*, 19 Mar. 1836.
10 CSORPPI, Carlow 1835, Hugh
    Murray to Sub-Inspector, 31 July 1835.
11 Map illustrative of the different routes
    between Borris, Kilgraney and
    Carrignafecka for the Trial of A. Sly,
    drafted by Charles Forth. CSORPPI,
    Carlow, 1835, 1053; *CS*, 8 Aug. 1835;
    Morning Chronicle, 17 Oct. 1837.
12 Samuel Lewis, *A topographical dictionary
    of Ireland* (2 vols, London, 1838), i, pp
    99, 216, 258. The police barracks
    nearest to Kilgraney was at Borris,
    accommodating 30 men, and there was
    a smaller station at Bagenalstown.
13 *Pigot's Commercial Directory of Ireland,
    1824* (London, 1824), p. 140.
14 *CS*, 12 Apr. 1834; Richard McMahon,
    'The courts of petty sessions and
    society in pre-Famine Galway' in R.
    Gillespie (ed.), *The re-making of modern

    Ireland: essays in honour of J.C. Beckett*
    (Dublin, 2003), pp 101–37.
15 CSORPPI, Carlow, 1835, 2/203,
    Joseph Green, Kilkenny, to Dublin
    Castle, 28 June 1835; 3/203, Sir John
    Harvey to Dublin Castle, 27 June
    1835; 4/203 Memorial of Carlow
    Freeholders, no date but filed with
    3/203.
16 *CS*, 24 October 1835, 21 Mar. 1836.
17 CSORPOR, Carlow 1835, 955/3, 24
    September 1835; *CS*, 22 Aug., 12 Sept.
    1835.
18 *FJ*, 3, 5, 10, 18 Aug. 1835, 18 Mar. 1836.
19 *FJ*, 3 Aug. 1835; *Examiner* (London), 9
    Aug. 1835.
20 CSORPPI, Carlow, 1835, 4/1053,
    Moloney to Dublin Castle, 11 Aug.
    1835.
21 CSORPPI, Carlow, 1835, 17/1053,
    Moloney to Dublin Castle, 26 Aug.
    1835.
22 *CS*, 24 October 1835, 21 Mar. 1836.
23 CSORPPI, Carlow, 1835, 203/1/3:
    Report of Constable Hugh Murray to
    Dublin Castle, 31 July 1835; *CS*, 15
    Aug. 1835
24 *CS*, 8 Aug. 1835; *FJ*, 19, 21 Mar. 1836.
25 *FJ*, 10 Aug. 1835; *CS*, 8, 15 Aug. 1835.
26 *Belfast Newsletter*, 4 Aug. 1835, 25 Mar.
    1836; *Darby Mercury*, 4 Nov. 1835;
    Ipswich Journal, 2 April 1836; *Indiana
    Journal*, 20 Aug. 1836; *Morning Chronicle*,
    25 Mar., 17 Oct. 1837; *Hull Packet*, 3
    Aug. 1838; *Times*, 10 Aug., 1 Sept., 27
    Oct., 17 Dec. 1835, 16 Feb., 22, 24 Mar.,
    13 July 1836, 14 April 1837, 7 Aug.
    1839, *Times*, 10 Aug., 1 Sept., 27 Oct.,
    17 Dec. 1835, 16 Feb., 22, 24 Mar., 13
    July 1836, 14 Apr. 1837, 7 Aug. 1839.

3. PROCURING EVIDENCE

1   *FJ*, 21 Mar. 1836.
2   CSORPPI, Carlow 1835, 203/1/3,
    Draft indictment for the murder of
    Revd John Walsh. Evidence of
    Matthew Murphy, 14 Jan. 1836.
3   Catherine Ann Power, 'The origins
    and development of Bagenalstown,
    c.1680–1920' in Thomas McGrath
    (ed.), *Carlow: history and society:*

interdisciplinary essays on the history of an
Irish County (Dublin, 2008), pp 424;
CS, 22 Aug. 1835 quoting *Kilkenny*
Moderator.

4   NLI, MS 29,778 (3), List of persons
    who voted for Col. Bruen and Mr
    Kavanagh at the January election 1835
    and who voted against them at the
    June election 1835: (4) Notebook
    with alphabetical list of all voters in
    Idrone West and East and St Mullins.
    Record of their votes January and June
    1835.

5   *CS,* 8 Aug. 1835, 19 Mar. 1836; *FJ,* 21
    Mar. 1836.

6   This was Michael Murphy, a
    substantial Catholic farmer, who was
    also actively involved in subscribing to
    the 'Beresford Fund' organized in
    1832 to protect Protestant farmers
    who were subject to attack. Power,
    'Origins and development of
    Bagenalstown', p. 425.

7   *FJ,* 10 Aug. 1835.

8   *CS,* 28 Aug. 1835.

9   CSORPPI, Carlow 1835/1053,
    203/1/3, Voluntary Confession of John
    Broderick, 12 Oct. 1835; 1053/20,
    Moloney, stipendiary magistrate,
    Bagenalstown, to Dublin Castle, 12
    Oct. 1835; *CS,* 29 Aug. 1835.

10 *CS,* 24, 31 Oct. 1835.

11 CSORPPI, Carlow 1835, 5/1053,
    Murder. 600 Pounds Reward – Poster,
    14 Aug. 1835; 10/1053. Moloney to
    Dublin Castle, 15 Aug. 1835.

12 *CS,* 19 Mar. 1836.

13 CSORPPI, Carlow 1835, 13/1053.
    Sworn statement of Anne Rooney, 22
    Aug. 1835.

14 CSORPPI, Carlow 1835, 203/1/3.
    Sworn evidence of James Doyle, 6
    Oct. 1835.

15 *CS,* 19 Mar. 1836.

16 CSORPPI, Carlow 1835, 203/1/3,
    Sworn evidence of Patrick Fleming,
    26 Feb. 1836; *CS,* 19 Mar. 1836.

17 CSORPPI, Carlow 1835, 203/1/3,
    Dockets of consultations, Carlow
    Assizes 1836, Examination of Sub-
    Constable Corrigan, 17 Nov. 1835; *FJ,*
    23 Mar. 1836.

18 CSORPPI, Carlow 1835, 16/1053,
    Report of Moloney, Resident

    Magistrate, to Dublin Castle, 28 Aug
    1835; *FJ,* 23 Mar. 1836.

19 *FJ,* 2 Sept. 1835.

20 CSORPPI, Carlow 1835, 203/1/3,
    Dockets of consultations, Carlow
    Assizes 1836.

21 *CS,* 19 Mar. 1836.

22 *CS,* 19 Mar. 1836.

23 CSORPPI, Carlow 1835, 14/1053,
    Papers connected with the case of
    Archibald Sly tried for the murder of
    Revd John Walsh in 1836; 1835/1053,
    203/1/3, Correspondence between
    Drummond et. al. and Attorney
    General, 9, 18 Feb. 1836.

24 CSORPPI, Carlow 1835/1053,
    203/1/3.Geale, Crown Solicitor to
    Attorney General, Maryborough, 12
    Mar. 1836.

25 Elizabeth Malcolm, 'The reign of
    terror in Carlow: the politics of
    policing Ireland in the late 1830s', *Irish*
    Historical Studies, 32:125 (May 2000),
    64; *Times,* 23 Aug. 1839.

26 *FJ,* 21 Mar, 1836.

27 *Times,* 10 Aug. 1835.

28 CSORPPI, Carlow 1835, 1053/16.
    Moloney to Dublin Castle, 26 Aug.
    1835; *FJ,* 23 Mar. 1836.

29 *FJ,* 21 Mar. 1836.

30 *CS,* 19 Mar. 1836.

31 CSORPPI, Carlow 1835, 1053/23.
    Petition from Francis Patterson to
    Castle against his dismissal from police,
    Mar. 1836, no day given.

32 CSORPPI, Carlow, 1835, 203/1/3,
    Sworn statement of Patrick Fleming,
    26 Feb. 1836.

33 CSORPPI, Carlow 1835, 25/1053.
    Walter Moloney to Viscount Morpeth,
    26 Nov. 1835.

34 *CS,* 27 June 1835; CSORPPI, Carlow
    1835, 7/1053, 15 Aug. 1835.

35 CSORPPI, Carlow 1835, 4/203,
    Memorial from Carlow inhabitants, no
    date but after 27 June 1835; 1835,
    203/1/15. Barker Thacker,
    Ballymeelish to Dublin Castle, 6 July
    1835; *Report from the select committee*
    appointed to inquire into the nature,
    character and extent of orange lodges,
    associations or societies in Ireland: with the
    minutes of evidence, and appendix.,
    appendix to the report, p. 44.

36 CSORPPI, Carlow 1835, 6/210, 7/210, 10/210, 15, 16 Aug. 1835.

37 *CS*, 14 Nov. 1835.

38 CSORPPI, Carlow 1836, Memorial of Francise Patterson, 23 Mar. 1836; 1836, 3/612/33, Memorial to Lord Mulgrave from Kiledmond.

39 CSORPPI, Carlow 1835, 1053, 203/1/3, Edward Geale, Crown Solicitor to Attorney General, 12 Mar. 1836; 1053/14, Papers connected with the case of Archibald Sly tried for the murder of the Revd John Walsh in 1836, McCredy and Bate, Attorneys, to Dublin Castle, 9 Mar. 1836; *FJ*, 21 Mar. 1836.

40 W.E. Vaughan, *Murder trials in Ireland, 1836–1914* (Dublin, 2009), p. 139.

41 *FJ*, 21 Mar. 1836, 24 Aug. 1839. The jurors challenged by Sly and put aside were William Maher, T. Haughton, M. Kelly, John Nowlan, James Lyons, Thomas Donnohoe, E. Cullen, M. Dowling and Thomas Connell.

42 *CS*, 23 Mar. 1836; *FJ*, 21 Mar. 1836, 24 Aug. 1839; CSORPPI, Carlow, 1835/1053, 203/1/3, Geale, Crown Solicitor, to Drummond, 24 June 1836. The Protestant jurors were Henry Newton, Henry Carey, William Tennant, Henry Dyer, John L. Watson, William Young, Gabriel Thorpe, Stanley Johnson, Adam B. Feltus, Robert Carter and Edmund Murrow. The Catholic juror was Mr P. Finn.

43 Vaughan, *Murder trials*, p. 120.

44 *FJ*, 23 Mar. 1836.

45 CSORPPI, Carlow 1835, 103/19. Walter Newton to Drummond, 7 Aug. 1835.

46 Corrigan was dismissed from the police force immediately Sly's trial was over. Registered Papers 1836/34/35, Police Dismissals, 23 Mar. 1836.

47 CSORPPI, Carlow 1835/1053, 203/1/3, Geale, Crown Solicitor to Drummond, 24 June 1836.

48 *CS*, 19 Mar. 1835.

49 CSORPPI, Carlow 1835/1053, 203/1/3, Alexander McDonald to Drummond, 20 June 1836; 1053/9, Revd James Maher to Drummond 2, 13 Oct. 1836.

4. GREAT HATRED, LITTLE ROOM

1 Malcolm, 'Reign of terror', pp 65–8.

2 Isaac Slater, *National Commercial Directory of Ireland including … alphabetical directories of Dublin, Belfast, Cork and Limerick* (Manchester, 1846), p. 10.

3 CSORPPI, Carlow 1835, 12/1053. Moloney, Bagenalstown, to Dublin Castle, 20 Aug. 1835.

4 Galen Broeker, *Rural disorder and police reform in Ireland, 1812–1836* (London, 1970), pp 229–31; SOC, Carlow, 1824/2603, 7, 20 Nov. 1824; *CS*, 31 Oct. 1835; CSORPPI, Carlow 1836/305.

5 CSORPPI, Carlow 1835, 3/203 Sir John Harvey to Dublin Castle, 27 June 1835.

6 *Leinster Independent*, 20 June 1835.

7 *Pigot's Commercial Directory of Ireland*, 1824, p. 22; Slater, *National Commercial Directory 1846*, pp 10, 22.

8 *Minutes of evidence taken before the select committee on bribery at elections*, H.C. 1835 (547), Evidence of Revd James Maher, Qs. 9868–9869, p. 362; *CS*, 17 June, 19 Sept. 1835.

9 Lewis, *Topographical dictionary*, i, p. 216; *Kilkenny Journal*, 2 Apr. 1836.

10 *CS*, 1 February, 26 Apr. 1834.

11 *Evidence taken before the parliamentary commissioners to inquire into the occupation of land in Ireland* (referred to hereafter as *Devon Commission*), evidence of Captain Robert Owen, agent to Lord Courtown, Qs. 68, 154–5, pp 133, 141.

12 *CS*, 2, 9 Aug. 1834.

13 Power, 'The origins and development of Bagenalstown', pp 422–4; *CS*, 2 Aug. 1834.

14 Donal McCartney, 'Parliamentary representation and electoral politics in Carlow' in Thomas McGrath (ed.), *Carlow: history and society* (Dublin, 2008), pp 495–596; Malcolm, 'Reign of terror', pp 62–4.

15 Brian Walker, *Parliamentary election results in Ireland, 1801–1922* (Dublin, 1978), pp 200, 256–7, 331–2. The town of Carlow returned a single

representative to parliament over the same period, with some of the same names as held the county seats figuring among the representatives.

16 The population of Carlow county in 1831 was approximately 72,564, and the electorate was 1,246. Walker, *Parliamentary Election Results*, p. 256. *Devon Commission*, evidence of Captain Robert Owen, agent to Lord Courtown, Qs. 64, p. 133; McCartney, 'Parliamentary representation', pp 495–596.

17 *Leinster Independent*, 20 June 1835; *CS*, 25 April 1835.

18 *Minutes of evidence before the select committee on bribery at elections*, Evidence of James Byrne, Qs. 8191–8200, p. 469; Murphy, *The Fathers Walsh*, pp 9–17.

19 *CS*, 27 June 1835; *Borris Chapels. Copies of Correspondence between the Roman Catholic priests of Borris, Robert Doyne, Esq and the Lord Lieutenant of Ireland, on the alleged attendance of the military at the Roman Catholic chapels*. H.C. 1835 (198), xlv. 493, p. 4.

20 NLI, MS. 29,778,(5) Lord Courtown to his Catholic tenants in Barrahaskin, Ballinvally, Ballybrack, Knockamore, Knockroe, Sliedoordy, 25 Nov. 1840.

21 John Ryan, *The history and antiquities of the county of Carlow* (Dublin, 1833), pp 356–75.

22 *CS*, 30 Aug. 1834, 24 Jan. 1835.

23 NLI MS 29,778 (1), List of Freeholders 1830; *Report of the Committee on the Carlow Election Petition*, Qs. 504–5, p. 39, Qs. 534, p. 40; *Griffith's Valuation*, county of Carlow, parish of Ardristan, townland of Roscat, pp 100–1; *CS*, 15 Aug. 1835; *Kilkenny Journal*, 2 Apr. 1836.

24 *Devon Commission*, evidence of Captain Robert Owen, Qs. 64–65, p. 133.

25 *CS*, 4 July 1835.

26 *CS*, 10 May 1834, 25 July 1835; CSORPOR, Carlow, 1835, 7/135, 7 Jan. 1835.

27 McCartney, 'Parliamentary representation', pp 496–7.

28 Power, 'Origins and Development of Bagenalstown', p. 424.

29 *CS*, 15, 22, 29 Aug. 1835.

30 Murphy, *The Fathers Walsh*, pp 71–7; *CS*, 24 Jan. 1835.

31 CSORPOR, Carlow, 1835, 9/107, 8 Feb. 1835; 15/107, 24 Jan. 1835.

32 CSORPOR, Carlow, 1835, 11/107, 8 Feb. 1835; 13/107, 6 Feb. 1835; *CS*, 31 Jan. 1835.

33 CSORPPI, Carlow 1835, 107/2/21, Joseph Greene to Sir William Gosset

34 *FJ*, 31 July 1835; *CS*, 8, 15, 22 Aug. 1835.

35 *FJ*, 28 Mar. 1836.

36 *CS*, 4 May 1836.

37 Desmond Keenan, 'Ireland 1800–1850: General Election December 1834–January 1835', Carlow County, Ireland Genealogical Projects, http://www.igp-web.com/carlow/General_election_34_35.htm, accessed 17 Apr. 2010.

38 *CS*, 18 July, 17, 24 Oct, 7 Nov. 1835; Desmond Bowen, *The Protestant crusade in Ireland* (Dublin, 1978), pp 74–5, 99–103.

39 *Times*, 24 Mar. 1836.

40 CSORPPI, Carlow 1835, 107/3/20, Sir John Harvey to Dublin Castle, 23 June 1835.

41 SOC, 1822, 2634, 14 Jan. 1822; *CS*, 4 May 1836.

42 *CS*, 29 June 1834.

43 *CS*, 30 Aug. 1834.

44 *CS*, 1 Feb., 5 Apr. 1834.

45 *Indiana Journal*, 20 Aug. 1836; Murphy, *The Fathers Walsh*, p. 18; *Report from the Select Committee on Bribery at Elections, together with the minutes of evidence, appendix and index*. H.C., 1835 (547), Qs. 8197–8202, p. 469, Evidence of James Byrne.

46 CSORPOR, Carlow, 1835, 9/107, 8 Feb. 1835; *Borris Chapels. Copies of Correspondence between the Roman Catholic priests of Borris, Robert Doyne, Esq and the Lord Lieutenant of Ireland, on the alleged attendance of the military at the Roman Catholic chapels*. H.C. 1835 (198), xlv. 493, pp 3–6.

47 *Borris Chapels. Copies of Correspondence*, pp 1–2.

48 CSORPPI, Carlow 1835, 9/107, 8 Feb. 1835.

49 *Borris Chapels. Copies of Correspondence*, pp 4–6.

50 *CS*, 20 June 1835; CSORPPI, Carlow, 1835, 1953/23, Mar. 1836 (no day given).
51 *CS*, 25, 27 July 1835.

5. FINDING A SCAPEGOAT

1 Lewis, *Topographical dictionary*, i, p. 255; Slater, *National commercial directory of Ireland*, 1846, p. 10. The population of the county was calculated as 78,952 in 1821, 81,988 in 1831, and 86,228 in 1841.
2 *Devon Commission*, evidence of Captain Robert Owen, Qs. 11, 379, pp 131, 134; Lewis, *Topographical dictionary*, i, p. 259.
3 R. Timothy Campbell and Stephen Boyle, 'The country house and its demesne in Co. Carlow', in McGrath (ed.), *Carlow history and society*, p. 738; NLI MS 29,778 (6): Amount of arrears due on Carlow Estates 25 Mar. 1841.
4 *Devon Commission*, Evidence of Captain Robert Owen, Qs. 116, 118, 120, 134, pp 135–40; NLI, MS 29,778 (1), Comments on condition and tenure.
5 *CS*, 1 Feb. 1834; Lewis, *Topographical dictionary*, i, p. 259.
6 Power, 'Origins and development of Bagenalstown', p. 425.
7 *Devon Commission*, evidence of Captain Robert Owen, agent to Lord Courtown in Carlow, Qs. 32, 36, pp 132–3.
8 *CS*, 2 May 1835.
9 *Devon Commission*, Evidence of Captain Robert Owen, Qs. 27, 35, 39, p. 132; *CS*, 4 May 1836.
10 *FJ*, 17 Aug. 1839.
11 CSORPOR, Carlow, 1835, 7/135 (7 Jan. 1835), 28A/3 (24 June 1835), 54/3 (7 Dec. 1835); *CS*, 4 May 1836. One group evicted in Ballinabranna consisted of five separate households comprising a widow and her daughter, and the families of her sister-in-law, her son-in-law and her two sons.
12 *CS*, 5 Apr. 1832; Donal McCartney, *The dawning of democracy: Ireland, 1800–1870* (Dublin, 1987), pp 130–43.

13 *Papers relating to the state of Ireland, Province of Leinster, Return of Outrages, County of Carlow. H.C. 1834 (459), p. 68.* CSORPOR, Carlow, 1835, 7/135, 7 Jan. 1835; 28A/3, 24 June 1835; CSORPPI, Carlow 1835, 107/1, James Battersby to Sir John Harvey, 5 July 1835.
14 *CS*, 27 June 1835.
15 *CS*, 29 Aug. 1835; *Hull Packet*, 3 Aug. 1838.
16 SOC, Carlow, 1824/2603, 6 Oct. 1824; Bowen, *The Protestant crusade*, p. 100.
17 *CS*, 27 June 1835.
18 SOC, 1798, 1017/3, 28 May, 12 June 1798; *CS*, 2 Aug. 1834; Maura Duggan, 'United Irishmen, Orangemen and the 1798 Rebellion in Co. Carlow' in McGrath (ed.), *Carlow: history and society*, p. 565.
19 CSORPOR, Carlow, 1835, 955/3, 24 Sept 1835.
20 *CS*, 2 Aug. 1834, 27 June 1835.
21 CSORPPI, Carlow 1836, 203/1/3, Walter Moloney, Castlecomer to Piers Geale, 21 Feb. 1836.
22 Broeker, *Rural disorder*, pp 219, 234–8; *Peace Preservation Force, Ireland. H.C. 1834 (201) xlvii, p. 10.* The Peace Preservation Force stationed at Carlow Graigue had numbered 10 in 1832 but had been reduced to 5 the following year; *CS*, 25 July 1835.
23 *CS*, 27 June 1835; CSORPPI, Carlow 1836, 203/1/1 Walter Molony, Castlecomer to Drummond, 25 February 1836; 1835/1053, 23 Mar. 1836. Petition from Francis Patterson, Police Constable, to Dublin Castle, regarding his dismissal from the force, Nov. 1835.
24 *CS*, 7 Nov. 1835.
25 *CS*, 24 Oct., 7 Nov. 1835.
26 *Devon Commission*, evidence of Captain Robert Owen, Qs. 29, 75, 77, pp 132, 134. The fifth farmer benefiting from the clearances was one of the original smallholders.
27 Power, 'Origins and development of Bagenalstown', pp 424–5.
28 *Griffith's Primary Valuation of Tenements*, Province of Leinster, county of Carlow, parish of Lorum, townland of Sliguff, p. 244. The surnames in

question were James, Agar, Young, Hughes, Kidd, Watkins, Tyndall, Styles, Wynne, Hatton, Malcolmson, Burrowes, Williams, and Roberts. It is difficult to be certain as to the denomination in every case, especially since similar surnames listed for the region in the 1911 census were actually Catholic.

29 Pat Purcell Papers, 'Disturbers of the Peace', Carlow County, Ireland Genealogical Projects, http://www. igp-web.com/Carlow/ PP_papers_ 27.htm, accessed 18 Feb. 2010.

30 *CS*, 25 Apr. 1835.

31 Power, 'Origins and development of Bagenalstown', p. 424.

32 NLI, MS 29,778, 3, List per persons who voted for Col. Bruen and Mr Kavanagh at the January election 1835 and who voted against them at the June election 1835, and Freeholders who would not vote for you although they had promised you to do so; 6, Amount of arrears due to you by the following persons to 25 Mar. 1841; *Kilkenny Journal*, 2 Apr. 1836.

33 *CS*, 4 May 1836.

34 CSORPOR, Carlow, 1835, 7/135, 7 Jan. 1835; 54/3, 7 Dec. 1835.

35 *CS*, 20 June 1835.

36 NLI, MS 29,778 (6), Law procedures taken.

37 Power, 'Origins and development of Bagenalstown', p. 425. Murphy leased 205 acres in Sliguffand 35 in nearby Ballyellen.

38 CSORPPI, Carlow, 1835, 5/1053, 14 Aug. 1835.

39 Gun Licences 1832–6, Names of persons in Carlow, Ireland, to whom a licence for arms has been granted. Carlow County – Ireland Genealogical Projects, http://www.igp-web.com/carlow/ Gun_Licences.htm, accessed 18 Feb. 2010.

40 *CS*, 20 June 1835

41 CSORPPI, Carlow, 1836/224, 2 Aug. 1836, Moloney to Drummond.

42 Broeker, *Rural disorder*, p. 222; *CS*, 5 Sept. 1835.

43 Duggan, 'United Irishmen', pp 557, 561. Duggan identifies the lodges in

1798 as being located in Rathvilly, Clogrenan, Agharue, Garryhill, Clonegal and Tullow.

44 CSORPPI, Carlow, 1836/214/1. Walter Moloney, Castlecomer to Drummond, 13 July 1836.

45 CSORPPI, Carlow, 1836, 231/1, Major Miller to Dublin Castle, 16 Aug. 1836, 6 Nov. 1836; Hereward Senior, *Orangeism in Ireland and Britain, 1795–1836* (London, 1966), p. 273;. Broeker, *Rural disorder*, p. 226.

46 CSORPPI, Carlow 1835, 3/203, 4/203, Memorial from freeholders of county and town and Carlow relative to Orange presence at Carlow election.

47 CSORPPI, Carlow 1835, 203. Correspondence between William Hamilton, Peafield, Borris-in-Ossory and other Queen's Co. gentlemen, Colonel J. Rochfort of Clogrenan, Carlow, and Dublin Castle, 30 May 1835 to 6 July 1835 regarding 'Orange Processions' in Carlow.

48 McMahon, 'Courts of petty sessions', pp 110–16.

49 CSORPPI, Carlow 1835, 203/1/14: J.S. Rochfort, JP Carlow and Queen's County to Dublin Castle.

50 *Report from the select committee appointed to inquire into the nature, character, extent and tendency of orange lodges, associations or societies in Ireland; with the minutes of evidence, and appendix*, H.C. 1835 (377). Evidence of earl of Gosford, Qs. 4026, p. 281; Evidence of S.V. Stoven, Qs. 4718 p. 339; *Second report from the Select Committee appointed to inquire into the nature, character, extent and tendency of orange lodges, associations or societies in Ireland; with the minutes of evidence, and appendix*. H.C. 1835 (475) (476), Appendix to the report, pp 30, 40.

51 CSORPPI, Carlow 1836, 3/612, 33. (Box 52), no date but 1836; *CS*, 25 May 1835.

52 *CS*, 19 Mar. 1836.

53 *A return of the number of troops or corps of effective yeomanry regiments or troops of volunteers*, H.C. 1821 (306), p. 4; *Yeomanry and Volunteer Corps, return of effective yeomanry and expense of each corps in the United Kingdom, for the year*

1833, with an abstract of sums voted and expended from 1816 to 1834, H.C. 1834 (67) XLII, 89, p. 4; *Kilkenny Journal,* 3 July 1836.

54 Duggan, 'United Irishmen', p. 556.

55 Broeker, *Rural disorder,* pp 209, 230; *Kilkenny Journal,* 3 July 1836;

56 *Kilkenny Journal,* 3 July 1836; *Wexford assizes – Newtown Barry. Copies of indictments against Captain Graham; and copies of informations and depositions, on the subject matter of the indictments, transmitted to the Crown Office of the county of Wexford,* H.C. 1831 (221), pp 7, 8, 13, 26.

57 *FJ,* 19 Mar. 1836.

58 Pat Purcell Papers, 'Disturbers of the peace', Carlow County, Ireland Genealogical Projects, http://www.igp-web.com/Carlow/PP_papers_27.htm, accessed 18 Feb. 2010.

59 *FJ,* 23 Mar. 1837.

60 *Morning Chronicle,* 17 Oct. 1837.

61 *CS,* 19, 21 Mar. 1836.

62 *FJ,* 21 Mar. 1836, 23 Mar. 1837.

6. INTO THE FUTURE

1 *Kilkenny Journal,* 3 July 1836. There is no record of Fleming in the Transportation Registers, so this report was probably accurate. Convict Reference Files (National Archives of Ireland), 1836, D/101; Transportation Registers (National Archives of Ireland), Tr. 1, 1836, p. 16; Irish Convicts to New South Wales 1788–1849, provided by Peter Mayberry, http://members.tip.net.au/~ppmav/cg i-bin/irish/irish.cgi (accessed 2 Feb. 2010).

2 *Hull Packet,* 3 Aug. 1838.

3 *CS,* 8 Oct. 1836.

4 *Griffith's Valuation,* Province of Leinster, County Carlow, Parish of Fennagh, p. 221.

5 Murphy, *The Fathers Walsh,* p. 277, suggests that Sly went to Scotland, but if, as the newspapers estimated, he was a man of 50 in 1834, he was quite elderly by the early 1850s when the primary valuation was completed; National Archives of Ireland, Census of Ireland 1911, County Carlow, Barony of Idrone West, Parish of Lorum, District Electoral Division of Sliguff, Form N, Enumerator's Abstract and Form B1, House and Building Return.

6 *FJ,* 21 June 1841, *Blackwood's Edinburgh Magazine,* 43 (1838), 813.

7 *FJ,* 21 June 1841.

8 *CS,* 12 Sept. 1835; *FJ,* 23 Mar. 1836.

9 Malcolm, 'Reign of terror', pp 61–6.

10 *Blackwood's Edinburgh Magazine,* 43 (1838), 812; *Fraser's Magazine for Town and Country,* 13 (Jan.–June 1836), 371; *Times,* 10 Aug. 1835, 24 Mar. 1836; *Belfast Newsletter,* 25 Mar. 1836; *Morning Chronicle,* 25 Mar. 1837; *FJ,* 24 Aug. 1839; *Hansard Parliamentary Debates,* house of lords' debate, 6 Aug. 1839, vol. 49, cols. 1305–1307; *CS,* 12 Sept. 1835; *Kilkenny Moderator,* 13 July 1836.

11 Point raised in conversation by Mr Michael Brennan of Carlow, 1 April 2010.

12 *CS,* 6 Jan. 1838.

CONCLUSION: REMEMBERING

1 *CS,* 24 Oct. 1835.

2 Wall tablet in Church of the Sacred Heart, Borris.